Miscellany poems by Tho. Heyrick ... (1691)

Thomas Heyrick

Miscellany poems by Tho. Heyrick ...

Poems.

Submarine voyage.

Heyrick, Thomas, d. 1694.

"The submarine voyage : a Pindarick poem in four parts ... 1691" has special t.p.

[2], xxii, 112, [4], 67 p.

Cambridge : Printed by John Hayes for the author, and are to be sold by Francis Hicks ... and by Thomas Basset ... and Samuel Heyrick ..., 1691.

Arber's Term cat. / II 336

Wing / H1753

English

Early English Books Online (EEBO) Editions

Imagine holding history in your hands.

Now you can. Digitally preserved and previously accessible only through libraries as Early English Books Online, this rare material is now available in single print editions. Thousands of books written between 1475 and 1700 and ranging from religion to astronomy, medicine to music, can be delivered to your doorstep in individual volumes of high-quality historical reproductions.

We have been compiling these historic treasures for more than 70 years. Long before such a thing as "digital" even existed, ProQuest founder Eugene Power began the noble task of preserving the British Museum's collection on microfilm. He then sought out other rare and endangered titles, providing unparalleled access to these works and collaborating with the world's top academic institutions to make them widely available for the first time. This project furthers that original vision.

These texts have now made the full journey -- from their original printing-press versions available only in rare-book rooms to online library access to new single volumes made possible by the partnership between artifact preservation and modern printing technology. A portion of the proceeds from every book sold supports the libraries and institutions that made this collection possible, and that still work to preserve these invaluable treasures passed down through time.

This is history, traveling through time since the dawn of printing to your own personal library.

Initial Proquest EEBO Print Editions collections include:

Early Literature

This comprehensive collection begins with the famous Elizabethan Era that saw such literary giants as Chaucer, Shakespeare and Marlowe, as well as the introduction of the sonnet. Traveling through Jacobean and Restoration literature, the highlight of this series is the Pollard and Redgrave 1475-1640 selection of the rarest works from the English Renaissance.

Early Documents of World History

This collection combines early English perspectives on world history with documentation of Parliament records, royal decrees and military documents that reveal the delicate balance of Church and State in early English government. For social historians, almanacs and calendars offer insight into daily life of common citizens. This exhaustively complete series presents a thorough picture of history through the English Civil War.

Historical Almanacs

Historically, almanacs served a variety of purposes from the more practical, such as planting and harvesting crops and plotting nautical routes, to predicting the future through the movements of the stars. This collection provides a wide range of consecutive years of "almanacks" and calendars that depict a vast array of everyday life as it was several hundred years ago.

Early History of Astronomy & Space

Humankind has studied the skies for centuries, seeking to find our place in the universe. Some of the most important discoveries in the field of astronomy were made in these texts recorded by ancient stargazers, but almost as impactful were the perspectives of those who considered their discoveries to be heresy. Any independent astronomer will find this an invaluable collection of titles arguing the truth of the cosmic system.

Early History of Industry & Science

Acting as a kind of historical Wall Street, this collection of industry manuals and records explores the thriving industries of construction; textile, especially wool and linen; salt; livestock; and many more.

Early English Wit, Poetry & Satire

The power of literary device was never more in its prime than during this period of history, where a wide array of political and religious satire mocked the status quo and poetry called humankind to transcend the rigors of daily life through love, God or principle. This series comments on historical patterns of the human condition that are still visible today.

Early English Drama & Theatre

This collection needs no introduction, combining the works of some of the greatest canonical writers of all time, including many plays composed for royalty such as Queen Elizabeth I and King Edward VI. In addition, this series includes history and criticism of drama, as well as examinations of technique.

Early History of Travel & Geography

Offering a fascinating view into the perception of the world during the sixteenth and seventeenth centuries, this collection includes accounts of Columbus's discovery of the Americas and encompasses most of the Age of Discovery, during which Europeans and their descendants intensively explored and mapped the world. This series is a wealth of information from some the most groundbreaking explorers.

Early Fables & Fairy Tales

This series includes many translations, some illustrated, of some of the most well-known mythologies of today, including Aesop's Fables and English fairy tales, as well as many Greek, Latin and even Oriental parables and criticism and interpretation on the subject.

Early Documents of Language & Linguistics

The evolution of English and foreign languages is documented in these original texts studying and recording early philology from the study of a variety of languages including Greek, Latin and Chinese, as well as multilingual volumes, to current slang and obscure words. Translations from Latin, Hebrew and Aramaic, grammar treatises and even dictionaries and guides to translation make this collection rich in cultures from around the world.

Early History of the Law

With extensive collections of land tenure and business law "forms" in Great Britain, this is a comprehensive resource for all kinds of early English legal precedents from feudal to constitutional law, Jewish and Jesuit law, laws about public finance to food supply and forestry, and even "immoral conditions." An abundance of law dictionaries, philosophy and history and criticism completes this series.

Early History of Kings, Queens and Royalty

This collection includes debates on the divine right of kings, royal statutes and proclamations, and political ballads and songs as related to a number of English kings and queens, with notable concentrations on foreign rulers King Louis IX and King Louis XIV of France, and King Philip II of Spain. Writings on ancient rulers and royal tradition focus on Scottish and Roman kings, Cleopatra and the Biblical kings Nebuchadnezzar and Solomon.

Early History of Love, Marriage & Sex

Human relationships intrigued and baffled thinkers and writers well before the postmodern age of psychology and self-help. Now readers can access the insights and intricacies of Anglo-Saxon interactions in sex and love, marriage and politics, and the truth that lies somewhere in between action and thought.

Early History of Medicine, Health & Disease

This series includes fascinating studies on the human brain from as early as the 16th century, as well as early studies on the physiological effects of tobacco use. Anatomy texts, medical treatises and wound treatment are also discussed, revealing the exponential development of medical theory and practice over more than two hundred years.

Early History of Logic, Science and Math

The "hard sciences" developed exponentially during the 16th and 17th centuries, both relying upon centuries of tradition and adding to the foundation of modern application, as is evidenced by this extensive collection. This is a rich collection of practical mathematics as applied to business, carpentry and geography as well as explorations of mathematical instruments and arithmetic; logic and logicians such as Aristotle and Socrates; and a number of scientific disciplines from natural history to physics.

Early History of Military, War and Weaponry

Any professional or amateur student of war will thrill at the untold riches in this collection of war theory and practice in the early Western World. The Age of Discovery and Enlightenment was also a time of great political and religious unrest, revealed in accounts of conflicts such as the Wars of the Roses.

Early History of Food

This collection combines the commercial aspects of food handling, preservation and supply to the more specific aspects of canning and preserving, meat carving, brewing beer and even candy-making with fruits and flowers, with a large resource of cookery and recipe books. Not to be forgotten is a "the great eater of Kent," a study in food habits.

Early History of Religion

From the beginning of recorded history we have looked to the heavens for inspiration and guidance. In these early religious documents, sermons, and pamphlets, we see the spiritual impact on the lives of both royalty and the commoner. We also get insights into a clergy that was growing ever more powerful as a political force. This is one of the world's largest collections of religious works of this type, revealing much about our interpretation of the modern church and spirituality.

Early Social Customs

Social customs, human interaction and leisure are the driving force of any culture. These unique and quirky works give us a glimpse of interesting aspects of day-to-day life as it existed in an earlier time. With books on games, sports, traditions, festivals, and hobbies it is one of the most fascinating collections in the series.

bibliolife
old books. new life.

MISCELLANY
POEMS.

By Tho. Heyrick, M. A. *Formerly of* Peter-*House College in* Cambridge.

Ἄνθρωπός ἐστι Ζῶον ἐπίπονον φύσει·
Παραψυχὰς οὖν φροντίδων ἀνεύρατο
Ταύτας,----*Timocles.*

CAMBRIDGE,
Printed by *John Hayes*, for the *Author*,
And are to be ſold by *Francis Hicks* Bookſeller in *Cambridge*,
And by *Thomas Baſſet* in *Fleetſtreet*, and *Samuel Heyrick* at
Greys-Inn Gate in *Holborn*, London. MDCXCI.

To the Right Honourable

KATHERINE Countess of *RUTLAND.*

May it Please Your Honour,

WHEN I first intended to Dedicate these *Poems* to Your Name, beside the Thoughts of their Unworthiness, I Was chiefly deterr'd by the Consideration of these Two Things, the Greatness of Your Quality and the Perspicuity of your Judgment: But then I was a little Encourag'd again, when I reflected, that the Meanest Creature was not debarr'd making Address to the Highest of Beings, but was rather commanded it; and that the Errours and Mistakes of well-meaning Men are likely to become rather the Pity, than the Scorn of Angels. Nor could I think it less, than a Natural Duty; that my humble *Muse* should offer the Best of Her Increase to that Family, to whose Bounty and Encouragement She ows all She is; since even the Gratefull *Indians* never Eat or Drink, till they have first powred out a Part as an Offering to that Bright Luminary, from whose Influence they believe, All, they receive, doth proceed.

I am very sensible and cannot but acknowledge, that there are many Things lyable to Exception in the Ensuing *Poems*; but they may well be Pardon'd, for the Sake of the *Beginning*, which is Consecrate to Your Name, and thereby receives a Peculiar Grace and Advantage, which cannot but diffuse it self thrô the whole Work. I confess even *there* what belongs to Me is full of Weakness; but it could be no otherwise, since in Subjects so Sublime, as Your Self, the most Towring Flights must of necessity flag, Things too High above Us not admitting a Definition; and as in Beauteous Faces there is something, We cannot Name, that exceeds the Pencil's Art, so in Excellent Personages there are Vertues, of which Common Souls have no Notion; but they Soar above the Description of the Loftiest Fancy. And surely no One is to be blam'd for going no farther; if He goes as far as the Subject will bear: For He is not ty'd to Impossibilities. And doubtless thô Poetry is usually suspected of Flattery, yet any One, who considers the Charms of Your Beauty, the Sharpness of Your Wit, the Depth of Your Judgment, the Candour of Your Temper, and Nobility of your Birth, will acknowledge, that You are plac'd above the reach of it; that, which would be Flattery to another, not measu-

measuring the least Part of Your Perfections; so that, if the Boldest and most Happy *Genius* should take the utmost bounds of Poetick Liberty in order to Praise Your Merit, He would find the Folly of his Attempt, and soon be forced with Confusion to give over the Impossible Design. For I suppose, there is None, but will grant, that the Highest Encomiums in Praise of the *Sun* are lost; every One having a Greater *Idea* of that Luminary than can be expreſs'd, and He is still as far above their Praise, as their Reach. Wherefore if Princes are best able to describe the secrets of Empire, Experienc'd Commanders matters of War, and Gallant Minds Heroick Vertues, I am inexcusably to blame, who have undertaken a Province too Difficult for Me to perform, and which requires the Pen of something more than a Man; which Crime I yet humbly beg Your Honour to forgive; since thô there may ly a Fault in my Ignorance and Rashness, yet, I am sure, there is none in the Design; since there is no One hath a Greater Zeal for the Glory of Your Honourable Family, than He, who is (MADAM)

Your most Humble

and Obliged Servant.

T. HEYRICK.

THE PREFACE To the READER.

I AM *sufficiently sensible under what Disadvantages these* Poems *come out, in which there is nothing either Profane, Obscene, or Seditious to recommend them, the usual Embellishments of Things of this Nature; in reference to which commonly the worse they are, the better they are accepted. Yet this I Studiously avoided, such Decorations neither agreeing with my Temper, nor Profession, and least of all with the Vertuous Character of that Illustrious Person, to whom they are Dedicated. Neither indeed was I willing to gratifie the profaneness of the A-* theist, *nor the ill-Nature of the Seditious, who love to feed their Eyes, as the Ancient* Romans *did on Bleeding* Gladiators: *Nor did I think it worth my while* to feed Swine. *There are certainly Subjects of Indifferency enow to employ a Man's leisure Hours, without medling with Thunderbolts, or Gibbets, or Diseases; and it requires no*

Great

Great Capacity to choose which is Best, either to live at Quiet and Peace, or have the Fate of an Ovid *or a* Cicero.

And since this is an Age of Politicks and every One pretends a Right, if not in Administring, yet at least in Censuring, the Government, I hope this may escape Censure-free, since it hath no Relation unto it; and if News is the thing, that is most acceptable, that which Men of all Estates gape after, and take upon Trust without examination, This Work of Mine, which consists of News too, and is (like much of that) pure Invention (for Poets *are not ty'd to the Rules of* Historians*) may receive favourable Entertainment. If it hath but its Turn, I am satisfied, thô afterwards it be confuted, for that is the Common Fate: And yet for ought I know, this may fare better, than is expected; for 'tis a* Poetical *Time; the Common Discourse and News-Letters are arrant* Romances *and Large Legends of Wandring Knights and the* Quixotes *of the Age. Men are* Poets, *thô they are not sensible of it, and Dote on the Ravings of their Own or Others Brains, thô they are wilder than the Centaurs, Giants, and Monsters, and all the* Chimæra's *of Antiquity. Men now adays want no* Invention *(one main Ingredient of* Poetry*) and if they do* Coherence, *'tis but imagining it* Pindarique, *and it goes off: As for* Probability, *'tis not much stood on in a Science, wherein every Thing goes down.*

The True Design of these Poems *was to draw Men's Minds, that are Idle, from more Dangerous, and as little profitable, Speculations: For Such, as have nothing to do, usually do what they should not, and are most Susceptible of Evil-Maxims against* Church *and* State: *And 'tis the custom of* Academies *to amuze Young Students Minds (which usually are hot and unbyass'd, have much of Sharpness and little of Solidity) with* Philosophy, *which thô it be confes-*

sedly,

sedly of great Use, yet one not the most Contemptible may be to bridle Young Wits from running too soon upon Divinity. *Those therefore, that are least able to* Judge, *being the most apt to* Censure *(as half-witted Men are always suspicious) my Design was to draw them to* Poetry, *which concerns them as much, as* Politicks *do, and that is Nothing at all; and to make them of the* Roman *Cobler's mind, who in a general Tumult upon the Death of* Cæsar *enquiring the News and being told, He was kill'd in the* Senate-*house, slunk into his Bulk again and cry'd,* He was a Cobler still. *For why should those Men, who see not upon what Center things turn round, think the Government is beholding to them for their Ridiculous Care? If I miss of my Design, I shall not much trouble my Self, many better Projects having come to Nothing; Things of Indifferency not being valued, but All esteem'd Good or Bad, as it pleases or displeases a Faction.*

To

To his Worthy Friend

Mr. THOMAS HEYRICK

on his Ingenious. Poems.

LONG hath the Sacred, Venerable, Name
Of POET (once so highly rais'd by Fame)
Been, nor unjustly, trampled under Feet;
Their *Laurels* blasted and their *Flowers* unsweet.
The Virgin Springs and Chaste *Pierian* Groves
Have been profan'd by Base Incestuous Loves:
Castalian Streams, so Pure in former Times,
Were since Polluted with unhallowed Rhymes:
When *Villains* durst the *Poet's* Task invade,
And Shamefull *Vice*, dress'd up in Masquerade,
Did Heavenly *Wit* presume to Personate:
While *Phœbus* and the *Nine* in Mourning sate.
Then Blushing *Vertue* never durst appear;
For Gaudy *Flatt'ry* her Rich Robes did wear.
Affrighted *Truth* fled the Enchanted Ground:
And *Chastity* could there no more be found:
False Fiends and Phantomes onely danc'd around.
What Shame and Grief did then our Souls oppress,
To see the *Laureate* Tribe in such Distress?
Vile *Mævius* Honour'd, *Maro* in Disgrace;
Loose *Sirens* seated in the *Muses* Place:
Wise *Fancy's* Sacred Flame extinguish'd quite;
While *Ignis Fatuus* shew'd a Cheating Light?
All were Asham'd, and All at This did Grieve! ----
But *Heyrick* only could Our Wrongs relieve.

He broke the Charm: *He* ended all the Spell:
And now th' Obſcener *Viſion's* fled to Hell.
Now Genuine *Senſe*, adorn'd with Manly Grace,
Doth ſhew to Heaven his Lov'd, Majeſtick, Face:
Now *Fancy's* various Mantle freely flows;
While Curious *Judgment* doth her Locks compoſe,
And braids in Artful Knots thoſe Treſſes fair,
That will the Hearts of *Phœbus's* Sons enſnare.
Now Charming *Wit*, which Few before did know,
Walks at Noon-day; doth all her Beauties ſhow,
How Sweet her Looks, how Raviſhing her Tongue,
What Heavenly Treaſure's in her Artfull Song:
How, while She innocently ſeeks to Pleaſe,
The Raviſh'd Soul forgets her old Diſeaſe,
And Painleſs Joys and Endleſs Pleaſures ſees.
   Thus to the Learned *Aragonian* King
That Health, which *Galen's* Art could never bring,
The Charming *Curtius* kindly did impart,
And Cur'd his Body, when He 'd Gain'd his Heart.
   Here wiſely-flowing *Eloquence* diſdains
To be confin'd, but in *Poetick* Chains:
Sweet are the Bonds, that tye the Soul to Senſe;
And ſcope allow for All things, but Offence!
   Here Various *Learning* doth her Wealth diſcloſe,
And All, that's worth our Knowledge, freely ſhows:
All *Nature's* Secrets offers to our View,
Far more, than Watry *Proteus* ever knew:
Thô *He* Great *Neptune's* ſcaly Herds doth keep,
Well-vers'd in All the Wonders of the Deep.
   For *Heyrick's* boundleſs and unwearied Mind
To this our Upper World can't be confin'd;
But ranſacks *Thetis's* Boſom and explores
Her Inmoſt Caverns and her Utmoſt Shores,

And ſtrangely doth the Vaſt *Abyſs* contain
Within the Vaſter *Ocean* of his Brain.
All, that was ever Writ, or Done, or Said,
Well hath He underſtood and well ſurvey'd:
Pierian Tempe, where *Apollo* Reigns,
And Spacious Hiſtory's Delightfull Plains,
And *Heaven* and *Earth's* far-diſtant Regions lie
Conſpicuous to his Sharp, Sagacious, Eye.
Nor yet meer Knowledge doth his Verſe beſtow;
But, as We're *Wiſer*, makes Us *Better* grow:
With *Moral* Uſe it ſmooths Rough *Nature's* Face,
And Human Art with Heavenly *Senſe* doth grace:
Vertue in every Lineament doth ſhine:
Groſs the *Materials*, but the *Form* Divine.
Yet, when my *Heyrick* would advance a Strain
Too High for All, that doth on Earth remain,
No *Female* Vanity, nor *Lordly* Ape,
Nor Wealthy *Ignorance*, nor Witleſs *Shape*,
Beſpeak his Muſe: ----But up aloft She flies,
And views Bright *VERTUE* with undazled Eyes:
On *Vertue* onely She delights to Gaze;
To *Vertue* onely gives Deſerved Praiſe:
For onely *Vertue*, and (which is the ſame,)
Great *RUTLAND*, can his Panegyricks claim; } (Name.
Chaſt *GAINSBOROW*, and the Heavenly *BRIDGET'S* }

Joſhua Barnes.

Emmanuel Coll. *Cambridge*
Novemb. 24. 1690.

 To

To my Ingenious Friend Mr. Heyrick, *Author of the* Submarine Voyage.

I.

LONG I in Darkneſs, by falſe Meteors led,
Have blindly follow'd *Truth*, that from me fled:
Long have purſu'd the harſh and rugged Road,
Where *Shakeſpear* and Great *Ben* before me trod:
Yet now, Dear Friend, in vain I find,
I did th' *Infatuating Fire* purſue;
It onely did amuſe my Mind,
And Me thrô Miſts and Labyrinths drew:
Dully thrô thick and thin I wander'd on,
O're *Denham's*, *Suckling's*, *Waller's* Poems ran;
And vainly thought my ſelf well Bleſt,
When I a while in *Cleaveland's* Shade could reſt;
And at his Fountain quench my Thirſt:
Or ſtretch'd my ſelf along that Current's ſide,
Which with a Natural Force
Directs its Courſe,
And all o're *Cowley's* Odes Divine doth glide.
Cowley, who firſt ſome faint Diſcovery made
Of *Pindar's* unknown Shore:
Who firſt did with *Anacreon* trade,
And came home laden with *Wit's* ſparkling Ore.
But You a more adventurous *Courſe* have ta'ne,
Which You alone were able to maintain
He dabled in the Straits of *Wit*, You lanch'd into the Main.

II.

Tell me, what Muſe Your Fancy doth inſpire
That I may now invoke the ſame?

Or

Or lend to Me Your Tunefull Lyre,
That I due Honours may proclaim ;
And while Your Praises I make known,
May Propagate my Own ;
And grow Immortal in the Mouth of Fame.
Lend me, O lend Your Quill,
Or Pardon, if against Your Will
I boldly do intrude
Among the numerous Multitude,
That to the Press with You do crowd.
In Pompous Dress You walk before in State,
And take Your Place in high *Apollo's* Court ;
While We, th' Inspired of the lower Sort,
Pay our Attendance at the Gate.

III.

On Your Officious *Dolphin's* Back
Thrô the vast Floods of *Time* I'le safely break :
Safely shall o're *Oblivion* ride
And stem th' Impetuous Current of her Tyde.
The fam'd *Arion* so had once been lost
And perish'd in the watry Brine,
Had not some *Dolphin*, kind like thine,
Convey'd him to the Coast.
Oh ! that my Numbers were like *His* ; that I,
Supported on Your Friendly Fin,
An unfrequented Voyage so might try,
Thrô Pearly, Chrystal, Paths might creep,
And sound the hidden Secrets of the Deep.
To *Neptune's* Palace might resort,
View all his Riches, all his Store,
Of Precious Gems and Golden Ore,
And wanton with his Beauteous *Nymphs* at Court.

IV.

What mighty Labour, mighty Pains
Some Poets take to wrack their Brains:
Small is their *Wit*, and much more ſmall their Gains.
One treads the Lofty *Stage*
To pleaſe the Humours of a vicious Age:
In *Satyr* there Another doth delight
That Malice, more than Praiſe, doth move.
Another ſofter Lays doth write,
And ſweats and travels in the Roads of *Love*.
But Your more Uſefull Muſe
Wiſely another Way doth choſe;
In mighty Numbers ſings
Of mighty Secrets, mighty Things:
Things, that are worthy of Your Generous Mind,
And advantagious unto all Mankind.

V.

You hidden Knowledge from the Deep do take,
As *Albemarle* redeem'd the Golden Wreck.
With ſo much Fancy all Your Truths are joyn'd,
So Gentle and ſo Sweet they goe,
So ſmoothly Ebb, ſo ſmoothly Flow,
At once they charm the Hearing, and inſtruct the Mind.
In ev'ry Line Your Genius is expreſt,
In ev'ry Word is found a lively Taſte
Both of the *Poet* and the *Prieſt*.
You in Your ſwift Poetick Flight
Sometimes do ſoar to a ſtupendious Height:
Sometimes do not diſdain
To Dive into the Main.
Your Odes may properly be ſtil'd Divine;
That both *Cæleſtial* are and *Submarine*.

VI. Judg

VI.

Judgement, and *Love*, what would ye doe?
Whither my willing Fancy drive?
In vain You whip, in vain You ſtrive,
In vain our Poet's Praiſe purſue:
So Bigg it looks, it's plac'd ſo High,
No human Art Acceſs can find;
We ſcarce can reach it with our Mind:
No Quill can to its Diſtance fly,
And Language laggs behind.
No wonder then, if ſunk beneath her Load
My Muſe declines the Road.
'Tis You alone to praiſe Your ſelf are fit,
But innate *Modeſty* is ſo
Predominant in You,
It bridles up Your Tongue and curbs Your Wit.

VII.

And yet, if I like *Dædalus* could fly
And ſoar with artfull Wings above the Sky:
Like him, could quit that deep and horrid Shade,
Shake off thoſe Chains
That clog my Brains,
Which Tyrant *Dulneſs* hath upon me laid:
I'de cut the yeilding Regions of the Air,
And o're Your Iſlands, o're Your *Ocean* ſteer,
And view thoſe watry Secrets, You have made ſo clear.
And thô perchance in my *Pindarick* Flight,
Rais'd to a too-ambitious Height,
The Fate of *Icarus* ſhould prove my Doom;
And angry *Phœbus* melt my waxen Plume:
Yet mine a much more glorious Lot would be,
Whilſt gently I ſhould drop into Your Sea,
Nor give the drowning Flood a Name, but take my Name (from Thee.

William Tunſtall.

To

Extended like a Love-sick Maid,
When she in pleasant Dreams doth grasp a Shade,
And wakes and sighs, because She is betray'd:
Not where the Jolly *Tritons* do resort
To talk of Love, of Business, or of Sport,
Where *Phœbus* blushing-red with Love, or Toil,
Doth hurry down the *Western* Hill,
To his Enjoyment, or his Rest,
And all o're *Cowley's* Odes Divine doth glide.
Cowley, who first some faint Discovery made
Of *Pindar's* unknown Shore:
Who first did with *Anacreon* trade,
And came home laden with rich sparkling Ore:
But Your more Adventurous *Course* have ta'ne,
Which You alone were able to maintain,
He dabled in the Straits of *Wit*, You lanch'd into the Main.

II.

Tell me, what Muse Your Fancy doth inspire
That I may now invoke the same?

Or

But surely, while those Depths You sweetly sing,
And charming Verse from the *Abyss* do bring
Such, as might rock the rattling Winds asleep,
And smooth the Angry Furrows of the Deep;
While *Venus*-like Your Lovely *Muse* doth rise
From Seas; and Storms themselves have something, doth surprise,
No single Name can all these Wonders shew,
But now You are *Arion* and the *Dolphin* too
[illegible]
Convey'd him to the Coast
Oh! that my Numbers were like *His*; that I,
Supported on Your Friendly Fin
An unfrequented Voyage I might try,
Thro' ev'ry [illegible] might creep
And sound the hidden Secrets of the Deep.
To *Nereus*'s Palace might resort,
View all his Riches, all his Store,
Of Precious Gems and Golden Ore,
And wanton with his Beauteous *Nymphs* at Court.

IV. Wha[t]

IV.

What mighty Labour, mighty Pains
Some Poets take to wrack their Brains?
Small is their *Wit*, and much more small their Gains.
One treads the Lofty *Stage*
To please the Humours of a vicious Age:
In *Satyr* there Another doth delight
That Malice, more than Praise, doth move.
Another softer Lays doth write,
And sweats and travels in the Roads of *Love*.
But Your more Usefull Muse
Wisely another Way doth chose;
In mighty Numbers sings
Of mighty Secrets, mighty Things:
Things, that are worthy of Your Generous Mind,
And advantagious unto all Mankind.

V.

You hidden Knowledge from the Deep do take,
As *Albemarle* redeem'd the Golden Wreck.
With so much Fancy all Your Truths are joyn'd,
So Gentle and so Sweet they goe,
So smoothly Ebb, so smoothly Flow,
At once they charm the Hearing, and instruct the Mind.
In ev'ry Line Your Genius is exprest,
In ev'ry Word is found a lively Taste
Both of the *Poet* and the *Priest*.
You in Your swift Poetick Flight
Sometimes do soar to a stupendious Height:
Sometimes do not disdain
To Dive into the Main.
Your Odes may properly be stil'd Divine;
That both *Cælestial* are and *Submarine*.

VI.

Judgement, and *Love*, what would ye doe?
Whither my willing Fancy drive?
In vain You whip, in vain You ſtrive,
In vain our Poet's Praiſe purſue:
So Bigg it looks, it's plac'd ſo High,
No human Art Acceſs can find;
We ſcarce can reach it with our Mind:
No Quill can to its Diſtance fly,
And Language laggs behind.
No wonder then, if ſunk beneath her Load
My Muſe declines the Road.
'Tis You alone to praiſe Your ſelf are fit,
But innate *Modeſty* is ſo
Predominant in You,
It bridles up Your Tongue and curbs Your Wit.

VII.

And yet, if I like *Dædalus* could fly
And ſoar with artfull Wings above the Sky:
Like him, could quit that deep and horrid Shade,
Shake off thoſe Chains
That clog my Brains,
Which Tyrant *Dulneſs* hath upon me laid:
I'de cut the yeilding Regions of the Air,
And o're Your Iſlands, o're Your *Ocean* ſteer,
And view thoſe watry Secrets, You have made ſo clear.
And thô perchance in my *Pindarick* Flight,
Rais'd to a too-ambit'ous Height,
The Fate of *Icarus* ſhould prove my Doom;
And angry *Phœbus* melt my waxen Plume:
Yet mine a much more glorious Lot would be,
Whilſt gently I ſhould drop into Your Sea, (from Thee.
Nor give the drowning Flood a Name, but take my Name

William Tunſtall.

To his Ingenious Friend, and Brother-Angler *Mr.* Thomas Heyrick *on his* Sub-marine Voyage, *&c.*

I.

HOW oft, where winding Rivers smil'd,
As they thrô flowry Meadows plaid;
Where Innocence and Pleasure made their Seat,
Secure, thô Low, and Happy, thô not Great,
Have we the well-spent Hours beguil'd?
Drank draughts of Joys, no bitter Griefs allay'd,
No Disappointments did invade?
Joys, *Pure*, as pearly Drops from Fountains rise,
Clear, as the *Chrystal* Streams, that charm'd our Eyes.
Free, as the *Choristers* of the Neighbouring Groves,
That in melodious Airs tun'd forth their Loves.
Smooth, as the Azure Heaven around us spread,
Or stealing Rills, that not one Murmur made.
No busie *Fiends* our Souls possess'd,
No dire *Ambition* seiz'd our Breast,
But fair *Content* lap'd up our Souls in Rest:
Not *Eastern* Monarchs half so blest!
Above vexatious Thoughts of being Great,
Contented with our Watry *Sphear*,
(For somtimes too a Rural Muse was there)
We rul'd our *Fortune*, and commanded *Fate*.

II.

These Happy Times are gone! Your tow'ring Mind
To such low Stations could not be confin'd,
You lanch'd into the Main, and left us far behind.

Follow

"Follow me Friends (You cry'd) where Honour calls us on
"And where Rewards our Induſtry will crown,
"The Gallant Mind new Continents deſcries,
"And Learned Souls make new Diſcoveries,
"While ſordid Moles hugg their ignoble Eaſe.
"The Bounds of the Dull *Stagyrite* wee'l paſs,
"Leave his dark hints behind:
"His Courſe *Euripus's* narrow Streams confin'd,
"And ſwallow'd up his fluctuating Mind.
"We'll rifle Virgin-undiſcover'd Seas,
"That may the *Learned* and *Ambitious* pleaſe,
"That will with *Knowledge* and with *Gold* abound;
"Till doubly We
"Are with *Victorious* and with *Learned* Laurels crown'd,
"And rule, what Kings fight to command, the *Sea*.
You ſpake, --but We were Deaf with *Fear*:
(For *Fear* and *Sloth* no brave Advice will hear)
Some laid in Eaſe refus'd to ſtirr,
Some the Sea's Surface did deterr:
The Boldeſt onely by the Shore durſt creep,
And *You* alone did ſtem the Terrours of the Deep.
We now too late our *Cowardiſe* deplore,
See *You* return'd with envy'd Store;
While *We*, (the due Reward of *Sloth*) are *Poor*.

III.

The Sea's now truly Free, You made it ſo;
Did thrô all Parts of that vaſt Empire go,
Nor miſs'd one dark Receſs.
Th' *Ocean's* no longer unconfin'd,
Nor the Sea Bottomleſs;
Nothing lies hid to Your inquiſitive Mind.
Not where the *Sea-Nymphs* dance and play,
Not where their weari'd Limbs they lay

Extended like a Love-sick Maid,
When she in pleasant Dreams doth grasp a Shade,
And wakes and sighs, because She is betray'd:
Not where the Jolly *Tritons* do resort
To talk of Love, of Business, or of Sport,
Where *Phœbus* blushing-red with Love, or Toil,
Doth hurry down the *Western* Hill,
To his Enjoyment, or his Rest,
T' unbend his Cares upon fair *Thetis's* Breast:
Or where Great *Neptune* doth his *Amphitrite* Court.
Nor can We tell, but You,
Who did so many Secrets know,
Some *Sea-Nymph* might, or *Goddess*, woe
And have your Assignations too below.

IV.

Pleasure and *Learning* in Your *Muse* are joyn'd:
You *Doubly* gratifie the Mind,
Delightfully and *Profitably* Kind.
To th' Curious *World* an *History* You give,
Which by no other Means *We* could receive;
(For all th' Inhabitants are Dumb below).
Which, as You've made *That* Great, will make *You* Live;
While *Fishes* cut the Waves, or *Waves* themselves do flow.
The Mighty *Whales* and Regal *Dolphins* there
Grow Big and Braver from your Artfull Pen;
The *Uranoscopus* forgets the Sphear,
And Charm'd by You begins to *look* on Men:
All *Neptune's* Court You've open'd to our View,
Adorn'd with Orient Pearl and Burnish'd Gold,
His Guard of *Tritons* and the Scaly Crew,
That in the watry Plains their Revels hold:
Which Glorious Objects do our Eyes detain,
While You our *Souls* do steal with your surprising Strain.

But

But surely, while those Depths You sweetly sing,
And charming Verse from the *Abyss* do bring
Such, as might rock the rattling Winds asleep,
And smooth the Angry Furrows of the Deep:
While *Venus*-like Your Lovely *Muse* doth rise (prise;
From Seas; and Storms themselves have something, doth sur-
No single Name can all these Wonders shew,
But now You are *Arion* and the *Dolphin* too.

V.

Your fatal Knowledge *Neptune* grieves in vain,
Laments, that e're he let a Spy
With treacherous Skill survey the watry Plain,
See where his Forts and Magazines do lie,
And (what Invasion tempts) his Treasury.
In vain the *Indians* do deplore
The *Spaniards* first Arrival on their Shore:
Once found, they were to all a Prey,
Discove'ry op'd to Slavery a way.
So doth a gloomy Fate hang o're the Sea,
If any dare so Hardy be
To trace the Steps of Your Discovery.
Such Difficulties overcome, we know,
Your Mind can't be confined long below :
Neptune already doth the Knowledge fear,
And's Brother *Jove* must doubly guard his Sphear.
A *Dolphin* You did through the Ocean goe,
And now a *Bird* of Paradise You'll be,
And all the Secrets o'th' Celestial Empire see.

Ribworth Septem. xi. 1690.

Theophilus Judd of St. *John's* College *Cambridge*.

To Mr. Heyrick *on his Excellent Poems.*

I.

N*Ature*, from whose Indulgent Hand
We all, that we esteem, do take,
Doth *Costly* Births of *Worthless* Matter make:
Doth Noble Forms upon them lay :
The charming Visions rise at her Command
Though their Materials be but *Dust* and *Clay*.
You greater Wonders to the World impart;
Your Learned Pen exceeds her Best of Art.
Her shapeless *Chaos* You anew Create,
Her Meanest Subjects from Your *Wit* grow Great.
Mortall, Imperfect, all her Products are:
Deathless You render them, and in *Perfection Fair*.

II.

The Proud *Pellæan* Youth, that *cry'd*----
Had *rav'd*, --More Worlds for to subdue,
Had he liv'd now, t' have been outdone by *You*.
Who scorn the Bounds, that Him confin'd,
Pass o're the *Rubicon*, his Arms defi'd,
And please with Wonders of the Deep *Your* Mind.
You once-Renowned *Drake's* Great Acts outdo;
He the *Gulph's* Surface, *You* its Bottom, view.
Bold *Curtius's* Deed with Yours runs Parallel;
Who scorn'd the *Acherontick* Jaws of Hell!
Both leap'd the *Gulph*, Both to the Gods were Dear;
You best-Belov'd, whom *They* and Ravenous *Seas* did spare.

III. Who

III.

Who then am I; that dare deviſe
With my Unhallowed Verſe to come,
Where Nobler *Muſes* are with Wonder Dumb :--
In vain We ſtrive to praiſe the *Sun*
Whoſe Worth above Expreſſion's Power doth riſe;
And's beſt by ſilent Adoration ſhown.----
The Mighty *B----s* can onely ſing Your Praiſe,
The Tunefull *B----s*, juſt Partner of Your Bays!
Great *Homer's* far-ſu[illegible]e to *Him* is due,
And *Pindar's* Song does ſeem reviv'd in *You* :
And ſurely He, that would ſuch Worth compriſe,
Muſt have a Soul, like Yours, *Great*, *Boundleſs*, *Sharp* & *Wiſe*.

George Walker of *Emmanuel* College in *Cambridge*.

To the Author on his Ingenious Submarine Voyage.

O D E.

I.

SAges *of old how vainly we admire* !
How fond's our Dotage on Antiquity !
Tho' their Short Sights could nought deſcry
Unobvious to each Vulgar Eye ;
The Idol'd Stagirite *could riſe no Higher*
Than the thin *Notion of* Hecceity :

When

When his more Prying Wit to' Euripus *flew,*
Its Famous Ebbs to view,
His Weaker Eyes
Us'd to the Dark Recess of Occult Qualities,
Could not Sustain Truth's *Glaring Light,*
Dazl'd with the Bright Miracle, He cry'd,
O Wondrous unintelligible Tide!
In what Dark Coverings art Thou involv'd,
Not by Entelechy's *or* Acts *resolv'd?*
Why do I on its Fruitless Surface gaze?——
Guide Me some Triton *thrô its Wandring Maze,*
Take Me (He cry'd) and with an Eager Leap
Plunges into the Swelling Deep.
Yet the Philosopher *no* Triton *found,*
But in the Rapid Stream was Drown'd:
What Fruitless Tryals then would He have made,
Had He the Boundless Depth essay'd!

II.

We'll no more Trophies to Columbus *raise,*
Nor to Vesputius's *stollen Praise:*
Too much We prize
Their mean Discoveries.
What has their Pregnant Wits brought forth
In the Long-expected Birth,
Beside the dull reiterated Scene of Earth?
Hurried by Storms, the unsought Ground
They rather Hapned on, than Found:
Those Random *Gusts the Praise must have,*
For a small Share our forc'd Discoverers can crave,
Who only were by Mechanism *brave.*
They in a Blind Neglect past by
Natures Great Excellence, Variety;

They

They could Discover nought worth Wonder there,
When Wafted round its Chrystal Hemisphere.
Whilst Your more prying Eye
Could not upon its Surface terminate,
Nor could the Loudest Storms Your Zealous Search abate.
You thrô Mæandrous *Caverns fearless rove,*
Discerning plainly in their Cause
The Ocean's *so-surprising Laws;*
While We above
Blind with Amazement do in vain,
Strive by Effects t' unfold the Cause's endless Train.
You Neptune's *Magazine have well survey'd,*
And thrô's Whole Watry Realm a Progress made.
Sure by some Amorous Syren *in Your way*
You were the Charms of Language taught;
She did impart.
With her Best Skill the Gracefull Art,
And by that Bribe would Mutual Flames have bought.

III.

The Mariner no more will Nature cruel call,
Thô He on Quicksands fall;
Thô Threatning Billows beat,
That on Sharp Rocks He split:
For taught by You none can a Shipwrack fear,
Thô Circumstantially *Severe:*
Since Sinking only does a Voyage *prove*
Into far Richer Scenes *of Life, than these above*
Go on, Bold Wit, and add to Nature's store,
All Her dark Nooks with curious search look o're:
Now into Her Remotest Corners pry,
And let no Lurking World escape Your Eye.
Rove thrô all Regions of the Sky,

And with ſome Agile crowd,
People that Vaſt Capacious Solitude :
Find where the Promptuary's of Fire are ſtow'd,
And in that Supermundial Heat
Room for ſome Cold Inhabitants create,
Search Nature thrô; till We no Blanks can ſee,
But find Her ſtretcht into Infinity.

Lancelot Manning, B. A. of *Trinity* College in *Cambridge.*

MISCEL

MISCELLANY POEMS.

On the Right Honourable John *Earl of* Rutland, *&c.*

OFF-ſpring of Hero's! Who art truly Great,
Above the reach of *pleas'd*, or *angry*, Fate;
And equally doſt ſcorn her *ſmile* and *hate*.
In Innocence and Vertuous Courage ſafe,
Above the World, You at its Troubles laugh:
Nor can its Pageantry attract your Eyes;
You fear not one, and th' other You deſpiſe.
A Life like this did *Atticus* commend,
The pride of glorious *Rome* and *Tully's* Friend,
Who 'n *Rome* none of its Civil wars did feel,
With no Commotions of the State did reel;
But in the world ſcarce with the World did deal.
"'Tis the world's Imperfection ſtill to want,
" And ſatisfaction, nor to have, nor grant;
" But with inceſſant pains to tear the Breaſt,
" And beg of every helpleſs Cauſe for reſt.
Angelick Natures our weak ſtate exceed,
Their *Purity's* from taint of Matter freed,
Their Knowledge no increaſe or growth doth need.
In this they moſt ſhow our confined ſtore;
They are ſo happy, they can wiſh no more.
Ambition is the Feaveriſh Soul's diſeaſe,
Which reſtleſs ſeeks for ſomething, that may pleaſe.

About with them their Malady they bear,
And wheresoe're they fly, they find it near,
And grope for help around and grasp the Air.
" *Content's* not there: He that doth strive for more
" Doth live uneasie with his present store.
" The wise Man doth Retirement's pleasures know,
" And's never less alone, than when he's so.
Fools are for nothing fit; the *Middle Size*
Drive on the Business of the world and Noise;
The *Highest* Souls to Nobler pleasures rise.
Out of the reach of Fortune they are plac'd,
Draughts of Sublime Æthereal Joys do tast,
Whom no Misfortunes break, nor Time doth wast
So *Adam* in his Paradise did live,
Bless'd in himself and his beloved *Eve*.
Er'e Glory drew unwary Eyes aside,
Er'e Gold did o'r'e the servile Troops preside:
And to all Mischief ope'd a passage wide.
Er'e glittering Courts Mens yielding Minds did sway,
Did all their tender precious Hours betray;
Whose loss not all their hopes and golden dreams could pay.
Er'e Men their Ease barter'd for Gold or State,
And sold themselves at an Unworthy rate:
Er'e Vice on Innocency's Tomb did grow: ----
Such is Your Life, and such a *Paradise* have You.
Who in Your Self find Native Inborn store,
Nor from the World do need to borrow more:
For he, that wants, thô ne'r so rich, is poor.
A scheme of Life, like Yours, *Lucretius* laid,
(Whose Boundless Wit all Nature's works survey'd)
And fitted to th' Immortal Gods, he made:
He gave them what would most Divinely please;
And lull'd them up in bless'd *Content* and *Ease*.

To

To the Right Honourable Katherine *Counteß of* Rutland.

THE Cautious Heathens, er'e they would admit
Their *Poets* of their *Deities* to treat,
First at their Altars made them Homage pay,
And purge their Dross and looser Strains away:
That the Exalted Purified mind
Might Notions fit for Heavenly Beings find.
So the bold *Artist*, that of You would speak,
Should Patterns from Celestial Natures take;
And stamp his Soul in an *Angelick* Mold;
Er'e he Your Vertues should attempt to' unfold.
In highest Sciences we words do want;
Expressions, that may give our Notions vent:
Thus *Rhet'rick* dumb at Your Perfections grows;
Our Language then, that 'tis defective, shows.
And thô those Flowers, which other Tongues refine,
She doth unto her Treasures wisely join;
All's yet too low for Subjects so Divine.
Homer the Language of the Heavens could tell,
Mysterious Secrets of the Gods reveal:
He that, how Good, or Great You are, would show,
Had need the Depth of Heavenly wisdom know:
For all we deal with here doth flag too low.
Angels the Mighty work should undertake,
And shew what Words they for such Merits make.
Had You liv'd in those Fabulous Ages, when
The *Heavenly* Seats held Colonies of *Men*;
When every Spark of Worth or Mounting Fire
Durst up into a *Deity* aspire;

What Deities had Your Perfections showd,
How many from Your Single Worth had flow'd?
Each Vertue had a God or Goddess given,
And You could from Your Self have peopled Heaven.
Nor to this Age alone extends Your Fame,
The Times to come shall spread Your Glorious Name.
And wheresoer'e the Name of *MANNERS* flies,
(A Name that doth all Excellence comprize)
As down the Ages it doth pass along,
You'l be the Subject of their Gratefull song:
And with Your Beauteous Offspring fix it fast,
Coëval with the World and Time to last.
And as Great *Cæsar's* haughty Name did come
Successively to all, that govern'd *Rome*;
Your Name, like Incence, shall descend to story,
And be the *Age's* Bliss and *Sexe's* Glory.
And all, whose Generous Breasts aspire to Fame,
With decent boldness shall assume Your Name,
Which in all Ages shall be understood
Significant for what is Great or Good.
Had but the Early Centuries, that could find
The Vertues and the Graces Woman-kind,
Seen the Fair Draughts of Your Celestial Mind:
New Sexes to their Deities they 'had given,
Nor left one Single God to rule in Heaven.

On the Lord Roos, *Eldest Son of the Earl of* Rutland.

WHen common Work for Painters hands doth call,
Rude artless Draughts do from their Pencils fall;

Adapted

Adapted to the judgment of the Crowd,
No Dancing Life doth make the Members proud:
But when a Celebrated Piece doth ſit,
For Wiſdom known, for Beauty, or for Wit;
The artfull ſtrokes do Life and Vigor breathe,
And ſteal an Immortality from Death.
So Nature, when the Common Herd ſhe makes,
Rough worthleſs Matter from baſe Rubbiſh takes:
Careleſs in any Shape ſhe molds the Clay,
No Beauteous Characters thereon doth lay:
To the Dull lump no coſt ſhe doth impart,
Courſe the Materials and as courſe the Art.
But when ſome Godlike Birth ſhe would improve,
That draws his Sparkling Line from Thundring *Jove*:
With her bright Seal ſhe ſtamps him for her own,
In dazling *Hieroglyphicks* writes him down.
For's *Body* takes Materials, fair as thoſe,
That do the Maſs of Common *Soul's* compoſe:
Fills it with every Vertue, every Grace,
And heavenly Beauties in the Mind doth place:
Vertues, that ſoar far above Common ken,
Known but to *Angels*, and *Seraphick* Men!
So *Nature*, Princely Youth, with you did deal,
With Excellence did Soul and Body fill:
And that it might not Caſual appear,
A Turn of Greatneſs and a Generous Air,
A ſhining S[illegible]it thrô the Whole did bear.
Rays, ſuch [illegible]s [illegible]own the Go[illegible]s, o're all did fly
And every [illegible] d breathe Divinity.
Others wi[illegible] te[illegible]ious ſteps to Vertue riſe.
Break to't thrô crowds of preſſing Enemies:
Muſt violence on headſtrong Nature lay,
Unhinge the Paſſions, er'e they will obey:

Which

Which, like tame Lions, if not rul'd by Art,
Will back into their Natural wildness start:
Like Countries, that but newly are subdu'd,
Will soon rebell and cast off Servitude.

Your Happy Mind inherent Vertue bears,
The Gift of Heaven and of Your Ancesters.
Others attain 't; an *Habit* 'tis in You,
What others do to Pains and Culture owe,
In Your Great Mind doth *Naturally* grow.
Your Family's Vertues so upon You wait,
It doth the Question put beyond debate,
That Parents Children's Souls do generate.
Grant blessed Heaven, Your Worth mayn't fatal be;
Nor too soon purchase Immortality! ---
And when Your Wisdom and Your Worth are known,
To th' world Your Candor and Your Goodness shown:
And when those Vertues, that to Age belong,
Shall in Your Youthfull Breast be found to throng:
Let not too soon bless'd Souls for You make room,
Nor *Death* believe You old and sign Your doom.

On an Indian *Tomineios, the Least of Birds.*

I.

IM'E made in sport by *Nature*, when
Shee's tir'd with the stupendious weight
Of forming *Elephants* and Beasts of State;
Rhinocerots, that love the Fen;
The *Elkes*, that scale the hills of Snow,
And *Lions* couching in their awfull Den:
These do work Nature hard, and then

Her wearied Hand in Me doth show,
What she can for her own Diversion doe.

II.

Man is a little World ('tis said)
And I in *Miniature* am drawn,
A Perfect Creature, but in Short-hand shown.
The *Ruck*, in *Madagascar* bred,
(If new Discoveries Truth do speak)
Whom greatest Beasts and armed Horsemen dread
Both Him and Me one Artist made:
Nature in this Delight doth take,
That can so Great and Little Monsters make.

III.

The *Indians* me a *Sunbeam* name,
And I may be the Child of one:
So small I am, my Kind is hardly known.
To some a sportive *Bird* I seem,
And some believe me but a *Fly*;
Thô me a Feather'd *Fowl* the Best esteem:
What er'e I am, I'me Nature's Gemm;
And, like a *Sunbeam* from the Sky,
I can't be follow'd by the quickest Eye.

IV.

I'me the true *Bird of Paradise*,
And heavenly Dew's my only Meat:
My Mouth so small, 'twill nothing else admit.
No Scales know how my weight to poise,
So Light, I seem condensed Air;
And did at th' End of the *Creation* rise,
When Nature wanted more Supplies,
When she could little Matter spare,
But in Return did make the work more *Rare*.

Claudian's *Eagle.*

THE *Eagle* doth not let his Eaglets rove,
Till th' Sun doth their Legitimacy prove.
When kindly heat doth the ripe Brood reveal,
And ſwelling Births do break the tender ſhell;
He turns his unfledg'd Off-ſpring to the sky,
And bids them look on Heaven with daring Eye.
Well the diſcerning Rays he views, to ſee
What will their Nature, Strength and Vigor be.
The Spurious Bird, that can't the Sunbeams bear,
His Father's Talons do in pieces tear:
But He, that views the Sun with daring ſight,
Nor ſhrinks at, what dazzles all elſe, the Light;
Nurs'd up with love becomes his Father's Heir
Deſtin'd the mighty *Thunderer* to bear.

The Fiſherman *and Treaſure.*

BEneath a ſhade, that overlook'd a Sea,
To whom a Chryſtal ſtream did Homage pay,
A Fiſher, arm'd with skill and patience, ſtood,
Whoſe Age beſpoke him Native of the flood:
By' whoſe Antick look and garb the Fiſh deceiv'd,
Him but a Tree's poor leafleſs Trunk believ'd:
Round whom the credulous Fry did fearleſs play,
While he with Specious baits did them betray.
It happ'd, as he his quiet Art employ'd,
Which him with Sport and Livelihood ſuppli'd,
Something far off did on a Billow ride:

And as he watch'd his Quill with patient care,
The moving Waves had brought the body near.
A lovely Youth, perhaps some Virgin's flame,
Perhaps his Father's joy, that should uphold his Name,
With mournfull *Miene*, to beg a Burial came.
The Aged Fisher the sad Object view'd
And doubly him with briny Tears bedew'd.
" Death makes a dreadfull change! perhaps (said he)
" Thou mightst the Favourite of some *Monarch* be:
" Nothing is spar'd by Death or by the Sea.
" Perhaps, said he, some Love-sick Maid doth wait
" Thy safe return, nor dreams of thy sad fate;
" Counts every Moment of thy tedious stay,
" And thinks each hour an Age doth bear away!
" To our own doom we'r Ignorant and blind,
" Much less, what haps to distant friends, can find.
" Perhaps —— alas, what may not we suppose;
" And yet what thoughts shall we in errour loose?
" Time past lyes hid, as well as Time to come,
" And we of both in vain enquire the doom.
" *Physiognomists* pretend events to tell,
" But can't, what hapned to the dead, reveal:
" Both unintelligible Mysteries ly,
" What *hath* been, or what *future* times shall be.
" That which is sure, is, thou dost want a Grave,
" The resting place indulgent *Nature* gave,
" That, which the Rich with all their Treasures buy,
" Nor Mother Earth doth to the Poor deny,
" Where Kings and Peasants, Spades and Scepters ly.
" Thy restless Soul wanders in devious ways,
" Not suffered the *Stygian* Lake to pass;
" While thy cold Members dance upon the Sea,
" And thy unburied Corps a prey doth ly.
" There is a debt we owe to all Mankind,

"Not to Relations or to Friends confin'd:
"The whole World in our kindness claims a share,
"And every One in need demands our Care.
"Thou nothing needest, and dost nothing crave,
"But, what's in all Mens power to give, a Grave.
"Riches I've none, nor dost thou need them now,
"That which I have I freely will bestow,
"A Grave is the last Favour I can show.
The Gods the Aged Man's intention heard,
And, that his piety they might reward,
Where he a Grave with trembling Members made,
A mass of Treasure underneath convey'd.
Vertue, that seldom her Reward doth gain,
But cloath'd in Rags despised doth remain,
While gilded *Vice* in costly State doth Reign,
Rich now by th' gift of Bounteous Heaven doth grow;
Who to th' mistaken World design'd to show,
What is to *Piety* and *Vertue* due.

On the Lady Bridget Noel.

WOnder of Nature! never yet
So bright a *Soul* and fair a *Body* met,
A *Jewell* worthy such a *Cabinet*:
Nature her gifts us'd *wisely to dispence*,
And with good Miene *supply the* Want of sence.
In You the stores of *Wit* and *Beauty* meet,
This Decks your *Face*, and that your *Mind*:
Heaven's Treasures are in You combin'd,
And every God with gifts your Birth did greet.

II. An

II.

Angels to You do brag they 'r kin,
Whose Soul doth thrô your Chrystal body shine;
And what appears without comes from within.
Your Body such, as Goddesses put on;
When they to meet their Earthly Loves come down.
Nature on You hath Lavish'd all her store,----
A Dearth of Beauty must succeed,
And Fools revolving Years must breed;
For *She*, that hath given all, can give no more.

Hippomenes and *Atalanta*.

WHen young *Hippomenes* beheld the place,
The ground, on which was run the fatal Race,
Where *Atalanta* should the Victor grace:
And saw their Members scatter'd o're the plain,
Whom Fate ordain'd to Love and to be slain;
Who paid their Life which in the Race did yield,
By fair, but cruell, *Atalanta* kill'd.——
"Is this the sole Reward, great *Love*, he cry'd,
"That doth to thy unhappy Slaves betide?
"Are these the Deities we must adore;
"That thus delight themselves in humane gore?
"If i'th the Æthereal Plains such Monsters be,
"Heaven shall be uninhabited for me.
"My bleeding Country shall my Aid demand,
"My Friend in danger shall require my hand,
"Actions like these beget a glorious Name,
"If i'th attempt I die, I die with Fame.
"These mangled Limbs were Men, that by their Hands
"Might have gain'd Crowns and conquer'd foreign Lands.

" But Love betray'd them,---Low in dust they sleep,
" And Ignominy o're their Names doth creep.
" They throve by *War*, were by soft *Love* undone,
" They well knew how to *stand*, but not to *run.*
" Hence then for ever I abjure the flame.—
—— But as he spoke, fair *Atalanta* came.—
A Bearded shaft did thrô his Liver dart:
And throbbing pain went tingling to his heart.
Silence seal'd up his lips, the sight took place,
The Valiant *Heart* bow'd to the charming *Face.*
Th' expanded Organ greedily receiv'd
Those piercing Looks, that him of rest bereav'd.
A secret Warmth thrô every Vein did glide,
And his Blood flow'd in an unusual tide.
In's Mind thoughts of untasted Joys did move
And sunk insensibly his Soul to Love.
His hardned Resolutions now expire,
And melt like rigid Ice before the Fire.
He now rejects the vows he once did make,
And thus, quite chang'd, his Words in Raptures brake
" Pardon, great Love, a Criminal, that ne're knew
" What was to Thee, or *Atalanta* due.
" And you (bless'd Souls) whom *Love* and *Beauty* slew
" I'll either Conquer, or make One of You.
" In bold Attempts 'tis gallant even to dare,
" For thô we miss the Prize, we Honour share.
" Show me the Post---I with Impatience dy,----
" My eager Love will double strength supply;
" And in the Race what warmth my breast will heat,
" To save a Life, and *Atalanta* get:
" All that I fear is, lest my throbbing heart,
" From her fair side unwillingly will part:
" It will be Lead, when it from Her is gone,
" *Nor can I from so great a Treasure run.*

" But if, at worst, the Fates my Bliss withstand,
" 'Twill be worth while to perish by her Hand.
" For since we once must yield to Destiny,
" By such an *Angel* who'd not wish to dy?
" Her *Eyes* can cure the wounds, her fair *Hand* gave,
" One Look of hers can ransom from the grave.

The Honourable Grazier.

THE *Roman* Heroes, that the World subdu'd
Both by their Candor and their Fortitude;
Did with their Arms as usefull Arts put on,
And Govern'd all by Moderation.
Conquer'd themselves, and then for Rule were fit;
Masters at Home, and then made All submit.
The spirit of Magistracy could put on,
And could without resentment lay it down.
Could in all states an even Temper show,
This day *Dictator* and the next at Plow.
So calmly you did bear the change of State,
Steer'd right the dangerous Ship of being Great,
Not swell'd with empty Gales of flattering Fate.
And when that needfull Maxims you did call,
From thence you gently did *descend*, not *fall*.
Your great Soul less employments stoop'd to bear,
As Gods sometimes to earthly seats repair.
Fate rules mean Souls, the brave do Fate command,
Who still unmov'd on their own Basis stand.
And should the World in pieces break, and all
The shatter'd ruines in one Tempest fall;
No fear could from the rowling Mountains rise,
Nor could their Innocence admit surprize.

"'Tis

" Tis the great Good, that we from Vertue gain ;
" Unmov'd in all Earth's changes to remain !

On a Peacock.

I.

THou foolish Bird, of Feathers proud,
Whose Lustre yet thine Eyes ne're see :
The gazing Wonder of the Crowd,
Beauteous, not to thy self, but Me !
Thy Hellish Voice doth those affright,
Whose Eyes were charmed at thy sight.

II.

Vainly thou think'st, those Eyes of thine
Were such as sleepy *Argus* lost ;
When he was touch'd with rod Divine,
Who late of Vigilance did boast.
Little at best they'll thee avail,
Not in thine *Head*, but in thy *Tayl.*

III.

Wisemen do *forward* look to try
What will in *following* Moments come :
Backward thy useless Eyes do ly,
Nor do enquire of *future* doom.
" Nothing can remedy what's past ;
" Wisedom must guard the present cast.

IV.

Our Eyes are best employ'd at home,
Not when they are on others plac'd :
From thine but little good can come,
Which never on thy self are cast :

What can of such a Tool be made?
A Tayl *well-furnish'd*, but an empty *Head.*

On a Flea *presented to a Lady, whose Breast it had bitten, in a* Golden *Wire,* Extempore. 1679. (*by Mr.* Joshua Barnes.)

-----HEre, Madam, take this Humble Slave,
Once vile,--But, since your blood is in him, Brave!
I saw him surfet on your Lovely Breast;
And snatch'd the Traytor from that precious Feast.
For his Attempt sure He by me had dy'd;
But the respect, I bore your Blood deny'd.
The Gods forbid, fair Madam, that by me
Your Blood be shed althô in this poor Flea!----
'Twas Sacrilege in him those Drops to draw;
But now that Treasure in his skin doth ly,
It consecrates his Life and strikes an awe;
That no bold Nayl dare make the Traytor dy.
Nay if a Quaff of *Nectar* once could make
Mankind Immortal, as the Poets feign,
This Flea can never dy for that Drops sake,
Which he hath suck'd, sweet Madam, from your Vein.
At least--no human Power his life can spill,
(Which lyes in your pure blood, that can't decay:)
But You, *whose Property's to save* and *kill*,
As you did lend that Blood, may take't away.
Then lo! --- this *Royal Slave* in chains of *Gold*,
Here I submit most humbly to your doom:
Either let *Mercy* him your Prisoner hold,
Or let your Ivory Nayl prepare his Tomb!

Oh!

Oh! could he ſpeak, I 'm ſure the Wretch would crave
  A *Priſoner's* life, to be confin'd with *You*:
Nay he could be content to meet his *Grave*;
  If by your Hand death might to him accrue.
Go, happy *Flea*! for now to One you go,
Gives *Bliſs*, if She 's your *Friend*, and *Glory*, if your *Foe*!

On an Ape.

I.

THIS Creature, that our Scorn doth grow,
Whoſe Actions we with laughter ſee,
Of Reaſon doth reſemblance ſhow,
And follows us with pleaſing Mimickry:
It aims at Wit; a Man would grow;
And would be *Rational*, if it knew how.

II.

'Tis more than We to *Angels* can;
Their Deeds we cannot Imitate:
We'er after all Endeavours *Man*;
Nor can we even in Shadow change our ſtate:
Nor what they are, or what they doe,
Can we but even in Show attain unto.

III.

Trifles our anxious Heads do fill,
Which this bleſs'd Creature trouble not:
Quarrels thence flow, the Cauſe of ill,
While Unconcern'dneſs is his happy Lot.
He is *our* Scorn, and much more W
The Scorn or Pitty may of *Angels* be.

IV. Like

IV.

Like *Man* ambitiously he acts,
While We in Paths of Beasts do tread;
Follow vain Fools in Vitious tracts,
And even to Hell are by Example led:
Great Aims his Mind doth *upward* call;
While basely We to what's *below* us crawl.

No to Morrow.

AN Holy Hermite, that to aged Years
His precious Moments had employ'd in Prayers;
Renew'd the Golden age, by Nature fed,
Took his Repose upon Earth's flowry Bed,
And had Heaven's Canopy above his Head:
With what was present did content his Mind,
And future things to Providence resign'd.
To Him some Friends did earnestly repair,
And begg'd at th' Consul's Choosing hee'd appear.
To whom Gray Hairs and Piety reply'd,
" What's in my power You shall not be deny'd.
" What You desire of me to Day I'le doe,
" But for to Morrow I can nothing show.
" You that are Young and hope for Future years,
" For times to come may fill your Heads with Cares.
" I use the Time is present; and no more,
" Than what to Day brings forth, account my store.
" I many Years have liv'd, yet never knew
" What was to Future Times and to *to Morrow* due.

Mart. *Lib.* 12. *Epig.* 23.

WHen Mony I on my bare Bond do crave,
Youv' none: I'le Mortgage, Sir,--oh! now you have.
Thus, *Theleſine*, you will not truſt a Friend,
But on the Credit of his Field You'l lend.
You'r caſt at Law; tell not me, tell my Land--
You want a Friend-- not I, my Field ſhall ſtand.

On the Crocodile.

I.

I AM the Terrour of the Sea,
Proud *Nile's* chief Glory and his Fear:
From far I dart upon my Prey,
Which to my watry Hold I bear.
Dogs dare not drink for doubt of Me,
Thô they 'gainſt Bulls and Lyons dare.
I am chief Inſtrument of Fate;
Two Elements upon me wait;
Water and *Land* conſpire to make me great.

II.

Of food I no Diſtinction make,
But in my Cruelty am Juſt:
Of Man and Beaſt alike I take,
And eat them both with equal Guſt.
With Draughts of Gore my thirſt I ſlake,
And Fleſh I down my throat do thruſt.
Fear gave riſe to Divinity;
And Gods haue roſe from Cruelty:
Wiſe *Ægypt* ſhowd ſo; when She worſhip'd me.

III. The

III.

The *Indians* kill me for their Food,
And say, I am Delicious meat:
They drink of their Relations Blood,
And eat, what did their Fathers eat.
In me they injure their own Brood,
Their Malice doth their Judgment cheat.
But I may yet a Question make,
Whether when Me they hunt and take,
They think their Hunger or Revenge to slake.

IV.

No Creature can my *Power* withstand:
Yet to that power *Deceit* I tie:
And by this Double *Gordian* band
Secure my hungry Tyranny;
The Terrour of the Sea and Land
In ambush on the Sands I lie.
What e're I take I do devour,
Yet o're the Head I tears do shower,
And weep and grieve, --because I have no more

V.

Men me Abhor, yet Imitate;
Like Falshood use without all Shame:
As Lawless Power, as deep Deceit
Doth *Christian* under *Christian* tame:
I live i'th' Actions of the Great;
What they're to Others, to them I am.
Would you then Power and Cunning see
Mixed with deep Hypocrisie?
They are conjoyn'd in *Man*, as well as *Me*!

On a Pen.

THE feather'd Herald of loud *Fame* I sing;
Love's sweetest Friend and *Satyr's* sharpest sting.
The fierce Denouncer of devouring Arms,
The soft Proposer of mild Peace's charms:
That o're the Troops of Proudest Monarchs sways,
That rules the Sword, which Heaven and Earth obeys:
That charm'd the Barbarous World, and brought the Rude
And Savage Troops from lonely Solitude:
That made them down in Peace togethet lie,
And molded them into Civility:
Their yeilding Hearts with secret Joy did move,
With tyes of Friendship and of mutual Love:
First shew'd the Service, we to Heaven did owe,
The Rev'rence we should unto Justice show,
And Rules of Converse, and what e're we know.
Earth's Distant parts the Nimble *Pen* doth bind,
And to remotest Nations bears the Mind.
Thou wondrous Gift of Heaven! that can'st dispence
Immortall favours and eternall Sence.
Thou to dark Ages dost full Luster give;
By Thee Great *Homer* and Great *Maro* live!
Those, we ne're saw, yet by thy Help we know;
And Friendship can at greatest distance show.
Thou needfull Rules for Government dost give,
And from Oppression dost the Weak relieve.
The Reins of all things in thy power do lie,
And He rules All, who well can govern Thee.
The peacefull Mind thou canst to War excite,
And sink the Warriour down into delight,

Great

Great Revolutions on thy power depend,
And Fates of Kings thy Motion do attend.
What secret spell doth in thy Letters ly?
What Magick Powers do from thy figures fly?
What wonders do the Savages relate
Of thine all-wise, all-wonderfull Estate?
That Characters, *which* from our Pens *do* stray,
To distant Climates should our thoughts convey.
Well might the *Indian* think the Letter spoke,
When by its help He in his theft was took.

On a Faithfull Dog.

MOST *Loyal Creature*! whom no Bribes can bend:
Still thou untaught thy Master dost defend.
Lov'st generous Actions, that will bear the Light,
Irreconcilable to deeds of Night.
To Thieves and Villains a professed Foe,
And what soe're doth hidden treachery know.
Ne're in distress didst leave thy wretched Lord,
But didst at Life's expence thy help afford.
From thy indulgent Master ne're didst fly,
Nor e're betray'd the hand, that nourish'd Thee.
But when all Loyal help is try'd in vain,
True and unmov'd dost by his side remain,
And dost thy Faith in Fates extreams maintain:
Well did the fierce * *Numidia*'s Prudent Lord
Choose from thy tribe his uncorrupted Guard.
Thy Life shames giddy *Man's*; for *He*'s a slave
To every Veering Wind and Dancing Wave.
Him Gold, or Spleen, or Flattery moves to range,
Or, what is worse, meerly the Love of change.

* *Masinissa*

He

He knows nor Gratitude, nor Honour's Laws,
But in extremity his help withdraws,
And leaves his Lord to th' mercy of his Foes.----
Villains or Fools the noiſy Crowds compoſe;
Or ſprightly Traytors, or dull ſtupid Logs;
How are they honour'd, if we ſtyle them *Dogs*?

On the Mole.

I.

BY Niggard unkind Nature I
Am doomed to perpetual Night;
In my dark ſolitude I ly,
And hate, what all do Love, the Light.
My days from nights no difference have,
But all my Life I'm in my Grave.

II.

I in Earth's bowels ſeek my prey,
In curſed ſolitude remain,
In thoſe dark Regions, where no Ray
May help to eaſe me of my pain:
Doubly accurs'd, that have no ſight,
Or, had I, am debarr'd the Light!

III.

Once I was an *Æthereal* mind
(If learn'd Antiquity ought know)
But cloy'd with Joys of Heavenly kind,
I long'd for Pleaſures here below:
Till angry Heaven from thence me thruſt,
And ſet my Manſion in the Duſt.

IV.

Now Blind, who once did Glory ſee,
And dwelt in the *Æthereal* Air:
From Heaven, and thoughts of it, I fly,
And do all Commerce with it fear.
In caverns deep my Seat I place,
And ſhun, as guilty men, Heaven's face.

V.

The ſtarting, trembling, Guilty Soul,
And Conſcience, that awake doth keep,
Might ſeek for ſhelter with the *Mole*;
And fix her habitation deep.
But tell me where a troubled mind,
A Dungeon deep enough ſhall find!

The Norway Whale.

I.

I Am the Meſſenger of angry Fate,
And do approaching Monarchs Death relate:
Norway with trembling Eyes doth look on me,
And I'me the Comet of the Sea.
Meteors from Heaven betoken Death,
And I do tell it from beneath.

II.

To Mariners an Iſland I appear,
And fearleſs they unto my ſide draw near,
Wondering what unknown Land their courſe doth ſtay,
And think they have miſtook their way.

Their

Their Charts and Mapps in vain they spread,
Believing Nature's lately brought to Bed.

III.

Yet wisely Nature with my Bulk doth deal,
And Folly on my Greatness doth entail;
Makes me a dull, stupid, and senceless Piece,
My Head but not my Brains encrease.
Did Wit or Malice dwell in me,
How dangerous a Monster should I be?

IV.

How many Whales may even our Country boast,
Whose Souls are in their Massy Bodies lost?
Who, if it haps they don't mischievous grow,
Their praise is, that they know not how:
Their Innocence from Folly got,
Their Excellence not in their Head, but Throat.

On Sleep.

SLeep, thou most soft and pleasing of the Gods,
That kindly easest weary Mortals Loads!
What other angry Deities infer,
Thou, Tutelary, *Genius* help'st to bear.
Even *Jove* himself must part the time with Thee,
Thou Ease and Aid of our Mortality!
To th' Gods and Fate we do the day resign,
But half the Time, the Night, sweet Sleep, is thine:
To whom our Life those Cordial hours doth owe,
Help to digest the Bitterness of woe!

The Springs of Life would soon exhausted be,
If not replenish'd and refresh'd by *Thee*.
Thou call'st the flagging Spirits to the Brain,
With Balmy Dew sprinklest the wearied Train,
That grow and flourish with thy moistning showers;
As silver Drops lift up the tender Flowers.
The long-distended Nerves are laid to rest,
And silent Ease spreads o're the heaving Breast:
A pleasing Numness on the Limbs doth seize,
And all, but Labouring *Fancy*, is at ease:
A thousand shapes She o're the Brain doth roul,
Disjointed Schemes play i'th' deluded Soul:
Inverted thoughts without, or Form, or Law,
Fragments of what before we heard, or saw:
Till the refreshed Spirits with haughty Pride,
With vigorous Strength thrô all the Limbs do glide,
And break the Silken Fetters, Sleep had ty'd.
Thou lull'st at once *Us* and our *Woes* asleep;
Thy Guards from Troubles faithfull Centry keep.
It is the sacred Time they must refrain,
And wait, till we rise from thy Arms again.
Thou Safe *Asylum*, where the wretched *Slave*
With the proud *Victor* equal share can have:
Both meet in thy Embraces, both lie down,
(I'th' *Grave* and *Sleep* there's no Distinction known)
Both sencelefs of the Joys, or Griefs, they own.
The weary *Wretch*, that Tugs at th' Oar doth find,
Of all the Gods, *Thou* art to him most kind.
Thy Charitable help doth condescend
Ease to the loaded Prisoner to lend,
That low in Dungeons lies far from the sight
Of Mortal Eyes, and th' common Good, the Light:
Thou cheer'st his blinded Eyes and troubled Mind,
And Him, that's lost to all the World, dost find.

Thou visit'st Humble Cotes and silent Cells,
Where Native *Innocence* and *Pleasure* dwells;
Where *Love* and *Peace* do undisturbed reign,
And *Truth* and *Safety*'s more esteem'd, than *Gain*.
But far thou fliest from *Courts* and *Rooms* of State,
From *Noise* of Business and of being Great.
Ambition there upon the Mind doth seize,
And *Lust* and *Rage* do rob the Soul of Ease:
Bloody *Revenge* the Tortur'd heart doth tear,
Nor doth black *Jealousie* the Entrails spare.
They smile without, but inwardly do bleed,
And restless *Vultures* on the Liver feed.
Scorpions and *Furies* there may make aboad,
But there's no Room for Thee, thou pleasing God!
With weary steps they may to *Honour* crawl,
And Golden showers into their Laps may fall:
But Thee they want, bless'd Sleep, who sweet'nest all.
All States and Tempers of thy Pleasures tast;
Which, when all other Joys are gone, do last.
Despairing Wretches, from whom Comforts fly,
May in Ambitious Dreams yet happy be,
And what they ne're shall have. Enjoy by Thee.
The Valiant *Souldier* dreams of Mortal Wars,
Of bloody Wounds and Honourable Scars,
Grasps at Imaginary Crowns, and lies
Entranc'd in Ravishing Sighs and Exstasies:
Till the soft Bonds of downy Sleep do break,
Then grieves and sighs, that he so soon doth wake.
A *Lover's* mind Beauteous Ideas dress,
While slumber doth his wandring Soul possess.
The Object of his Flame he doth adore,
Freely Embraces, what was Coy before,
What his unbounded thoughts desire, enjoys;
Fancy the room of what's not there supplies.

Unwil

Unwillingly he's wak'd out of his Dream,
And grieves, that all was but *Ixion*'s Scheme.
The sweet-tongu'd Poet, *whose Immortal Song*
Makes Men rise Gods, and Age it self grow young,
Tho poor Contempt offend his waking eyes,
Rich in thine Arms, thou Sole Mœcenas, *lyes.*
Sleep doth the Draughts of former Acts retrieve,
Disorder'd Cuts of Ancient Gests doth give:
Each of his Calling or his Deeds doth dream,
Merchants o'th' Sea, the *Husbandman* of's Team,
Lawyers of Strife, and *Sportsmen* of their Game.
Sleep theDay's Pleasures doubles in the Night,
And kindly represents what doth delight;
Death's younger Brother! --------
The first Essay of our Mortality;
The First, that learns us, what it is to dy!
A near agreement *Sleep* and *Death* do keep,
" Sleep's a short Death and Death a longer sleep.
In sleep our business with the World is done,
What's acted, or what's spoke, to us unknown:
Secret, as when we in the Grave lie down.
We'r unconcern'd at th' buz and Noise of things,
At the Erection or the fall of *Kings*.
No Plots nor deep Designs in hand we have,
Are but one step on this side of the Grave.
The *Dust* doth equal all, and *Sleep* doth so:
Alike to both, *Monarchs* and *Captives* bow:
While fast their sences sleepy Fetters bind,
No difference We 'twixt *Prince* and *Peasant* find;
All senceless Lumps of flesh alike; nor can
The *Wise* be sever'd from the *Foolish* Man.
Both may have Dreams, and both alike confus'd;
Chance governs all, where *Wisdom* is not us'd.

And *Peasants* may have Dreams as great and high,
As those that fill the head of *Majesty*.
They'r breathing Mummies all, and till they wake,
Wisdom or *Greatness* no Distinction make.

Martial's Ague. *Lib.* 10. *Ep.* 45.

IN sighs, *Leutinus*, thou dost spend the Days,
And wonder'st much so long thy Ague stays.
With Thee in gilded Coach it lolls at ease,
With Thee doth sup on far-fetch'd Rarities:
With Generous Liquor drunk it still is thine,
And knows no Water, but what cooles the Wine,
Crowned with Roses and with Perfumes spred,
Sleeps upon Down and rests on Purple Bed.
With Thee so entertain'd, what should it do?
Would'st have it to an half-starv'd Wretch to go?

Ætas parentum pejor avis tulit
Nos nequiores, mox daturos
Progeniem vitiosiorem. Hor.

WE all prize Life; and yet how short's the Date?
Not worth the trouble we are daily at.
Press'd with the load of Years, with Life we'r pleas'd,
With both our Arms, tho wretched, 'tis embrac'd.
Unhappy man! curs'd with a double Woe,
With Life's Vexation and its Shortness too.
How blessed was our uncorrupted State;
When from God's Hand we dropt Immaculate?

E're Nature had from Vice receiv'd its stain,
E're the Creation's *Glory* had its Bane.
When Moderation kept in drink and meat,
Men eat to Live, and did not Live to eat;
Before luxurious *Variety*
Had taught our Fathers Immature to dy.
When *Nature* open'd her unrifled store,
By former Ages never touch'd before,
Which flourish'd in its fresh unbafled Power.
When Native Knowledge o're the Soul was spread,
That could the use of *Herbs* and *Mettals* read,
And all, that might draw out Life's tender thread.
When benign Influences of the Stars
Contributed to Length of Happy Years,
That Those, who many Ages liv'd, might find
Those needfull Arts, of use to Humane kind.
We, of all Generations far the worst,
In Time, in Place, and in our Selves accurs'd,
In the gross *Lees* o'th' Elements do dwell,
With nauseous Air and putrid Matter swell:
A *Place*, refined Souls would think an *Hell*.
Where old Decrepit *Nature*, thrô Decay,
Doth feeble, weak, inglorious Births display;
Robb'd of her pristine store, the spirits fled,
The shortliv'd shadows withered Look and dead.
But yet the greatest and worst part of Woe,
Unhappy Man unto Himself doth owe!
We by our *Vice* our Natures do deprave,
We by *Intemperance* make too soon our Grave.
Passions do Knowledge blast and Reason blind,
And wear at once our Body and our *Mind*.
No wise designs for future times we lay,
Confin'd to the small Compass of *to day*.
Nature hath made us Wretched, but *We* more;
Fate curses us, and *we* add to the store.

Woes

Woes from our selves, or outward Causes, bred
With our own hands *We* pull down on our head.
A *Vertuous Life* would all these ills remove;
Our Nature, Years, and Knowledge, would improve;
Would render our short Lives more blest, and fair,
Than theirs, that did so many Ages wear.
This Life's in order to an *other* State,
The End and Crown doth upon *Death* await:
The Way to Happiness is thrô that Gate.
And in our Life it matters not to tell,
How many Years we've lived, but how Well.

Martial *Lib.* 9. *Ep.* 15.

DOST think, He whom thy liberal Table drew,
Can ever be to *Love* or *Friendship* true? ---
He loves thy Mullets, Oysters, and not *Thee*:
Could I so entertain him, hee'd love Me.

The Battle between a Cock *and a* Capon. Lamport 1682.

LET other Poets treat of lofty Things,
The rise of States and fall of Captive Kings:
A lower subject doth my Muse invite,
An humbler Theme, but of no less Delight.
A bloody Battle late was fought between
Two Combatants of different hopes and Meine.
One, the proud Captain of the brooding Race,
That doth the Yard o'th' carefull *Houswife* grace:
With tender Chuck calls the admiring Rout,
And proudly leads th' obsequious *Hens* about:

The

The drowsie Peasant's Clock, whose wakefull throat
Doth Midnight's shades and Day's approach denote:
Calls up from his course Bed the snoring Hind,
Whom Sleep's strong fetters do securely bind,
While guilty Greatness can no Quiet find.
The Creature, whom enjoyment can't appease,
But Raves in lust, and Rivals all his Race;
Not a *Seraglio* his Desires can please.
Impatient Lust doth in his Visage lie,
And deadly Rage dwells in his bloody Eye.
The *Other* of the Combatants was one
Of meaner hopes and expectation:
Not much unlike in shape, but much in Meine,
Nor Male, nor Female, but a sort between.
Monster! not made by Nature, but by Art;
Whose sex the carefull *Housewife* did impart:
Who conscious, *Lust* did fret the Nerves away,
And on Life's Balsame did too freely prey,
With bloody Knife did rob him of the prize,
Where *Love* is plac'd, and some say, *Courage* lies.
Angry with all the World for th' Inju'ry done,
A melancholly sullen Creature grown,
He Consort shuns, and loves to be alone.
Ghastly and pale he look'd, whether for fear,
Or rage at the Misfortunes, he did bear,
Or want of generous spirits and active fires,
Which daring uncontrouled Love inspires:
Each part unseemly look'd, but most of all
The bending Feathers of his useless *Tail*.
The Combat nois'd, to the unusual Sport
A gallant Train of Noble Youth resort.
All do the *Castrate's* sneaking looks deride,
And give their suffrage o'th' proud Champion's side.

Till

Till from the rest * *One*, born of noble Race,
Whom *Honour*, *Beauty*, *Wit*, and *Worth* did grace;
Whether it was his perspicacious Eye
Did growing sparks of hidden Valour spy;
(And who of Valour greater Judge than *He*?)
Or that he scorn'd to walk i'th' beaten road,
The common Path, that all the Vulgar trod;
Or that, as generous Spirits do, He chose
To lend his help unto the weaker cause,
As *Cato* did tho Gods did him oppose:
Castrate's Defence he took, and thus he spoke.
" *Narses* did once an Empire's fate revoke:
" Renown with Kingdoms he did bravely win.
" And Victory sat on his beardless Chin.
" *Europe* and *Asia* still deplore the fate,
" That *Sinan Bassa's* Valour did create!
" Both fill'd with Fame and Honourable scars;
" Unfit for *Venus*, fit for *Mars's* Wars.
O're *Castrate's* Soul the pleasing Accents spread,
And lifted up his long-dejected Head.
Great thoughts in his depressed Mind did grow,
And glowing Heat thrô every Limb did flow,
From valiant Race he sprung, (if Fame says true)
And his Descent from bloody Warriours drew:
Till Numerous Injuries and long Disgrace
(Scorn'd and contemn'd by all the female Race)
His high-born generous Spirit did debase.
But now swell'd up by Praise to bloody Fight,
Praise, that the Coward doth to Fame excite,
With deep Revenge his Soul doth inward bleed,
And Jealousie doth on his Liver feed,
A Jealousie from Impotence that's bred.
Rage, Madness, and Revenge his soul possess,
And his torn Heart to mighty Acts address.

* Sr Jo. [illegible]

Fierce

Fierce *Chanticleer* with haughty scornfull Pride
And mix'd Disdain over the Pit did stride,
And did th' Unworthy Combatant deride:
But, see'ing at last he did to fight prepare,
He gives the signal to th' unlucky Warr,
With that shrill Note, that ope's the *Morning's* Eye,
That dreadfull Note, that makes even *Lions* fly:
And with Revenge, which his proud Soul did swell,
He like a Tempest on his Enemy fell.
Both met, both others heightned Courage try'd,
And in deep Gore their shining Weapons died.
The Cautious *Castrate* let his eager Foe
In haughty Vaunts and scorn his strength bestow:
Disgrace and long-felt Shame had made him wise,
Taught him grave Arts and usefull Policies:
How to beguile a fierce and eager Foe,
How to ward off, and how return a Blow;
With circling winding Course his Foe deceive,
And deadly and unlook'd-for wounds to give.
To make his Enemie's fierceness useless still,
To fly and wound, and *Parthian-like* to kill.
With various fortune the event they try,
One doth on Force, th' other on Fraud rely,
And *Victory* with equal wings doth fly.
Besmeard with gore, with blood and fury red,
Blood they drink down, and showers of blood they shed.
With loss of blood at length the *Cock* grows faint,
And doth, too late, those fiery spirits want,
Which he so prodigally spent to please
The Lust of all his Speckled Mistresses:
Finds, what his glory was, his shame doth grow,
And *Lust*, that heightens, doth enervate too.
Yet scorning longer a base Foe to' engage,
He summons the remains of force and rage:

One blow he with united Forces made.
And *Castrate* senseless on the Pavement laid.
Netled with the Disgrace, brave *Castrate* rose:
Disgrace, that sparks of hidden Valour blows,
Ferments within, and wakes the sleeping seeds,
That many years lay dead, to gallant deeds.
All, that from Rage or wrankled Malice flow,
All, that Revenge or Jealousie can show,
All, that past Scorn, Disgrace, or biting Slight;
All in one fatal bloody Blow unite;
Which strow'd the *Cock* supinely on the ground,
While Blood and Life flow'd from the gaping wound.
Castrate on his fall'n Foe with pride did tread,
And lifting up his late-dejected Head,
He would have *Crow'd*, to show the Victory;
But barr'd by former wrongs that faculty,
He *Cackled* something out, which those, that know
The Tongue, he spoke in, do interpret so.
" Here the Insulting Conquerour doth lie,
" Mighty in *Venus* School, that could supply
" The Love of twenty *Hens*, and every Morn
" With fiery Lust his blushing Cheeks adorn.
"*Venus* and *Mars* have different ways of fight;
" One doth in *Love*, th' other in *Rage* delight:
" *Courage* resides i'th' noble seat the *Heart*;
" But *Love's* confin'd unto a *lower Part*.

Olympias's *Lamentation over Dead* Alexander.

VAin Youth! to what amounts now all thy Toil,
Or what Enjoyment hast thou of thy Spoil?

That

That, which with the Expence of sweat and blood
Thou dearly bought'st, is shar'd by th' wrangling Crowd.
Each on thy Spacious Empire sets his Eye,
And Thou neglected dost unburied ly.
Alive the trembling World to Thee did pray,
To Thee, now dead, none doth Obedience pay.
Thy former Deeds forgotten, by thy side
Thy fear, thy Reverence, and Authority did.
Nor could'st Thou, out of all thy Conquests, save
So much ground, as would serve Thee for a Grave.
The World but Yesterday thou thought'st too small,
And scorn'st the Narrow compass of this *Ball*:
Thy Towring thoughts and thy Designs laid low,
Seven foot of ground thy Burial place will grow;
But even that common Right thou wantest now.
Thy wild Ambition up to Heaven would soar,
Made servile Priests thy Altars to adore:
Alive thou we'rt inroll'd with Gods above,
But Death Thee truly did a Mortal prove:
Thy Death unravell'd all, thy Life had Wove.
Better, hot Boy, thou hadst in *Greece* remain'd,
And o're thy Native Land in quiet reign'd:
Than thus the peace o'th' Injur'd World to break,
And unjust Spoils from faultless Nations take:
And for thy Glorious Robberies, but to claim
The whole World's Curses and a *Posthume* Fame.

Big with great Schemes and flattering hopes we dy:
New crowding Numbers do the Soul employ,
While others swell up to Maturity:
Death closes up the Scene of Actions past,
And the imperfect *Embrio's* into Air do wast.

On a Robin-red-breast, *that for many years built and dwelt in a Church.*

I.

PRoud *Man* with high conceits doth swell,
And wonders of's own Worth doth tell:
Vainly believes, that he alone
Hath any Notion of *Religion.*
But they, blest Bird, that hear thy Songs, believe
The Truest Devotion in thy Breast doth live.
No *Envy*, *Pride*, or *Discontent* dwells there;
No factious *Interest*, mean Designs, or Fear,
Nor do *Hypocrisy* thy Actions wear.

II.

Angels are said their Prayers to Join
With holy Men in Acts Divine:
Thou mak'st the *Chorus*, when we pray,
And when we praise, thou sing'st thy cheerfull Lay.
To highest flights thy warm Devotion goes,
Thou op'st the Morning, and the Day dost close.
Thou by thy Carolls own'st a Deity,
To th' Altar dost for Sanctuary fly,
And wisest Men can only follow Thee.

III.

And if those Ancient Dreams be true,
That Souls thrô many changes go;
Some pious Mind, That wanted Rest,
Came and took up thy Zealous flaming Breast.

We

We here below with mists and Errours deal,
What Language Angels speak, there's none can tell;
Nor know we, but those Airs, that pleas'd our Soul,
That did in high *Seraphick* Numbers roul,
Might be some *Hallelujah*, Thou had'st stole.

On the Death of a Monkey.

I.

HEre *Busy* and yet *Innocent* lyes Dead,
Two things, that seldom meet:
No Plots nor Stratagems disturb'd his head,
Or's merry Soul did fret:
He shew'd like Superannuated *Peer*,
Grave was his look, and *Politick* his Air;
And he for *Nothing* too spent all his care.

II.

But that he died of Discontent, 'tis fear'd,
Head of the *Monkey* Rout;
To see so many Brother *Apes* preferr'd,
And he himself left out:
On all below he did his Anger showr,
Fit for a Court did all above adore,
H' had *Shows* of Reason, and few *Men* have more.

Advice to a Despairing Lover.

I.

WHY, silly Wretch, wil't pine and dy,
And unregarded ly?

Thou

Thou never sure did'st think to move
Either her Pitty, or her Love,
That's free from passion, like the Gods above.

II.

Let dy with Thee those hopes, that fed
These follies in thy head:
The *Sun* doth never cease to fly,
Nor th' *Moon* her wonted Course lays by,
Because a silly peevish Worm will dy.

III.

Monarchs may dy; and yet stern Fate
Flies at the wonted rate:
The Laws of Nature still wheel on,
And their unerring Course do run,
And no new grief doth stop their Motion.

IV.

Why then wilt thou resign thy Breath,
Since she minds not thy Death?
She, like the Stars, perhaps may see;
But plac'd in her Felicity,
She can't have sence of sorrow, or of *Thee*.

V.

Thou by thy Death wilt add one more,
One *Victim* to the Store,
And as those Heaps, in Battail slain,
Are known by Number, not by Name,
Thou nothing by thy Death, but Death shalt gain.

VI.

So do the unregarded Fry,
Like Beasts neglected dy;
And after some few Years of sleep
Oblivion o're their Names doth creep;
And their left Friends scarce their Remembrance keep.

Death's *Warning.*

A *Gallant* liv'd in Pride of Youthfull Powers,
Lull'd in soft Ease, bless'd Health, and tender hours:
Whose Easy Mind ne're ruffled was with Care,
Nor did the Toyl, or Load of Business bear:
Ne're knew Concern, but an Intreague of Love,
Nor beyond that amuzing Court did rove.
But stretch'd in shades he like an *Indian* lay,
To every smiling Moment's Birth did play,
And drank and danc'd and sang the Circling Years away.
To whom *Death* did in griezly shape appear,
Unerring *Death,* that doth to all repair,
Meets us in Beds of Down, as well as Fields of War.
Th' Officious *Fiend* doth on our footsteps tread,
Dresses in every Shape his hatefull Head,
As oft in what we Love, as what we dread.
The *Poor* beneath their troubles groaning dy,
The Rich expire in Exstasies of Joy:
The *Manner* differs, not the *Destiny.*
Th' Amazed *Spark,* struck with a cold surprize,
Who had with pleasing Objects fed his Eyes,
Found at the sight, wild Notions fill'd his head,
And all his Youthfull Warmth and Vigour fled,

Till

Till he, recover'd from his deep amaze,
Ask'd the *Grim Shape*, from whence, and what He was.
To whom the *Spectre* with insulting pride,
Lifting his Conquering Arm on high reply'd.----
" I'me the world's Monarch; to Me Princes bow,
" Scepters and Crowns do at my feet fall low.
" At my Command the suppliant Numbers come,
" And take their fixt inevitable Doom.
" All Creatures do beneath my Empire lie;
" And willing, or unwilling, they must die.
The Pointed Accents the Young Spark did hear,
Being already almost dead for fear;
And cry'd, " My tender Youth (great *Monarch*) spare.
" I am a feeble, unresisting, Prey,
" Too mean for your Victorious hand to slay.
" 'Twill sully all your former glorious Fame,
" To say, You such a Prostrate overcame.
" The rugged *Souldier* doth your force defie,
" And loudly calls on You, that from him fly.
" Dares you in your own Realm, the Scenes of blood,
" Where scatter'd Members o're the Fields are strow'd.
" The wretched *Prisoner* your Relief demands,
" And begs his wish'd-for Freedom from your hands,
" That can his fetters lose and break his Bands.
" Despairing *Lovers*, that no Joy do know,
" Do hope to find in You an End of Woe.
" You fly from those, that do defie your power,
" Are deaf to those, that do your Aid implore.---
" Humble the *Haughty*, with the *Wretch* comply;
" And let untouch'd the prostrate *Suppliant* lie.
Death seem'd to such a soft entreaty kind;
If ever he to Pitty was inclin'd,
(But Wisemen say, he's *Deaf*, as well as *Blind*.)

And told him, He his unripe Youth would ſpare,
But bad him for his next Approach prepare,
For he would then no vain excuſes hear.
Th' emboldned Youth acknowledg'd his high ſway,
And promis'd, his next Summons to obey;
But begg'd, he might have notice of the Day.
To whom *Death* cry'd, "You ſhall have what you crave,
"You ſhall of my Approach due warning have.
Glad of's Departure the Joy'd Youth aroſe,
Lapp'd his late frighted Soul in ſoft Repoſe:
Sang *Requiems* to his now-compoſed Mind,
Taſted each pleaſure, that look'd fair or kind:
Did ſet no bounds to' impetuous Deſire,
Freely embrac'd what Paſſion did require.
Ne're thought of *Death* more, or the threatned Grave
Which Melancholly dreadfull Proſpects gave,
But ſtill on this rely'd, *He ſhould a Warning have.*
No Preparations for's Departure made,
But to the Time of *Age* that Work delay'd,
And hop'd, that Debt ev'en then might be defray'd.
At laſt unlook'd-for *Death* approach did make
And him did from's enchanted ſlumber wake:
Who loudly at the Injury did rave,
And taxed *Death*, that he *no Warning gave.*
Who, ſmiling with a Grin, in Scorn reply'd,
"My Juſtice in all Ages hath been try'd:
"With equal feet to *Crowns* and *Spades* I come,
"None are *above*, none are *below*, my Doom.
"I've kept my promiſe; I fair *warning gave*,
"Each time you ſlept, I warn'd You of the Grave.
"*Sleep* is my Younger Brother, we dwell nigh;
"And there's but one ſtep betwixt Him and Me.
"I i'th' laſt *Feaver* did to you appear,
"And when the *Dropſie* ſeiz'd You, I was near.

" Your Nerves in *Lust* and in *Debauch'ry* broke,
" Your *Palsie* Hands in drunken Revels shook,
" Loudly with pressing signs did on You call:
" But You, regardless You, was Deaf to all.
" You scap'd before, and hop'd still so to doe,
" Far from your thoughts did drive the Day of Wo,
" You would not hear me call, nor will I you.
Th' Astonish'd *Youth* but little had to say,
And Death, who now refus'd to hear him Pray,
With one stroke even to *That* did stop the Way.

On a Sunbeam.

I.

THou Beauteous Off-spring of a Syre as Fair;
With thy kind Influence thou dost all things heat:
Thou gild'st the Heaven, the Sea, the Earth, and Air,
And under massy Rocks dost Gold beget.
Th' opaque dull *Earth* thou dost make fine,
Thou dost ith' *Moon* and *Planets* shine;
And if *Astronomy* say true,
Our *Earth* to them doth seem a *Planet* too.

II.

How unaccountable thy Journeys prove!
Thy swift Course thrô the Universe doth fly,
From lofty heights in distant Heavens above,
To all that at the lowly Center ly.
Thy Parent *Sun* once in a Day
Thrô Heaven doth steer his well-beat way;
Thou of a swifter subtler breed
Dost every *Moment* his *Day's* Course exceed.

III. Thy

III.

Thy Common preſence makes thee little priz'd,
Which if we once had loſt, wee'd dearly Buy:
How would the Blind hugg, what's by us deſpis'd
How welcome wouldſt thou in a *Dungeon* be?
Thrice-wretched thoſe, in Mines are bred,
That from thy ſight are buried,
When all the Stores, for which they try,
Neither in Uſe, nor Beauty, equal Thee.

IV.

Could there be found an Art to fix thee down,
And of condenſed Rays a Gem to make,
'Twould be the brighteſt Luſtre of a Crown,
And an eſteem invaluable take,
New Wars would the tir'd World moleſt,
And new *Ambition* fire Mens breaſt,
More Battels fought for it, than e're
Before for Love, Empire, or Treaſure, were.

V.

Thou'rt quickly born and doſt as quickly die:
Pitty ſo fair a Birth to fate ſhould fall!
Now here and now in abject Duſt doſt lie;
One Moment 'twixt thy Birth and Funeral.
Art thou, like *Angels*, only ſhown,
Then to our Grief for ever flown?
Tell me, *Apollo*, tell me where
The *Sunbeams* go, when they do diſappear.

The Athenian *Madman.*

I.

IN *Athens*, once the Nurse of Arms and Arts,
Where Wit and Learning fix'd their seat,
(Sometimes even there doth *Folly* meet,
For Nature variously her Gifts imparts:)
A *Madman* dwelt, the Laughter of the Town,
Who every Morning to the Port went down,
And thought all Ships, that enter'd, were his own.

II.

The Captains Hail'd, did for the Cockets call;
Enquir'd what Riches were on board,
What Merchandizes they had stor'd;
And what mishaps did in their Voyage fall.
Did his commands upon his servants lay;
To various parts the *Cargo* sent away,
To Merchants all, or storehouse, did convey.

III.

Nor was his (so dispis'd) a cursed state;
An Innocent *Madness* him doth seize,
A Frenzy, that his Mind doth please;
And uncontrouled thoughts upon him wait.
He thinks he's Happy and he's therefore so.
Believes he's Rich, and Wealth in Streams do flow:
He hugs the thought, *and thence doth blessed grow.*

IV. Ho

IV.

How many Men, than he, more raving are,
Who are amidſt their Treaſure poor,
And pine and ſtarve in ſwelling ſtore,
And might be happy, if they thought they were.
It is not Riches, that *Content* can win,
The ſecret we muſt to our heart reſign,
Content lives not without, but dwells within.

V.

We all alike do Happineſs deſire,
Yet commonly the Treaſure looſe:
The *Madman* doth, what's preſent chooſe,
He thinks no farther, nor doth more require.
Fancy makes him, what others fain would grow;
A ſerious Judgment doth ſmall difference know,
'Twixt *being* Happy, and 'twixt *thinking* ſo.

Martial's *happy Life.* Vitam quæ faciunt, &c. *Lib.* 10. *Ep.* 45.

WHat things our Life do happy make
From me, my ſweeteſt *Martial*, take.
A left *Eſtate*, not got with pain;
A fruitfull *Field*, that ſwells with grain;
A *Kitching*, that is ever warm;
Life free from Quarrels and from Harm.
Rarely to be concern'd with State,
Never to' have *Law-ſutes*, or debate;
But on the Mind *Content* to wait.

The

The *Strength* intire and *Body sound*,
And *Innocence* with *Prudence* crown'd:
An Equal and a Faithfull *Friend*,
Discourse, that may in *Pleasure* end,
Nor *Feasts*, that may to *Riot* tend.
No *drunken* Nights, yet *such*, as may
Wash off the sully of the Day.
No lonely *Bed*, yet One, that's *chast*;
And *Sleep*, that tedious Nights may wast.
With what we have to be *Content*,
Nor, what we have not, to resent:
Not fear our last approaching Day,
And yet not rashly fling our Life away.

Advice to a Virgin.

FAir blooming Beauty, left without defence,
Nothing to guard Thee, but thine Innocence!
Whose unexperienc'd Mind no ill doth know,
But Judges all things good, 'cause Thou art so.
Little thou think'st, what Dangers Thee surround,
What Plots and Stratagems laid under ground;
Which the fond Lovers, in thy Rays that play,
Against thy Innocent Designs do lay:
And thô they crouch beneath your sparkling Eyes,
Each boldly hopes, that You will be his Prize.
'Tis all great *Fortunes* and great *Beauties* get,
The *One* to buy th' *Other* to invite, *Deceit*.
For barren Countries none will ever fight,
'Tis the rich Soil the Conquest doth invite.
To gather common Stones no labour strives,
'Tis for rich Gems the Sun-burnt *Negro* dives.

Where

Where Plenty springs, or where rich Mines abound,
The Victory with due Rewards is Crown'd;
To Birds and Beasts is left the *Barren* ground.
Guard then your Beauty; 'tis a Dangerous Store,
A Fatal Treasure, that hath Ruin'd more,
Than e're were Wretched made by being poor.
Expect then often Storms; all are your Foes,
What e're their Countenance, or Behaviour shows,
That would possess those Treasures, You disclose.
Let *Vertue* Rule, and *Prudence* be your Guide,
All *Vice* and the *Suspicion* of't avoid.
Be Vertuous and be thought so; Few there be,
That dare attempt upon Your Chastity,
If no unwary Action did precede,
By which they gather'd hopes, they might Succeed.
" Fame's quickly lost and ne're to be retriev'd,
" And Rumour, true or false, blasts, if believ'd.
You're *Angels*, while You do admit no Stain;
But when You fall, You *Mortals* are again.
See that fair *Flower*, the Glory of the Field,
That did enchanting Joy and Pleasure yield,
By some rude Hand crop'd in its height of Pride;
How, all its Beauty fled, it withering died.
See but the *Snow*; like You, 'tis Starry bright,
While no warm touch doth taint its Native White:
But if ought doth its Virgin-Beauty stain,
Not all Earth's Treasures can restore't again.
Nor let (fair Piece of Nature) Your young Years
Be drawn away with Lovers vows and tears.
Love every Passion, it doth see, can *Ape*,
The changing *Proteus* puts on every shape.
Whom Love doth seize, he strait grows Eloquent,
And Streams of Words flow from desire and want;

Mind

Mind not the Trifles, on Mens lips that grow;
'Tis Scum, that from their boyling Breasts doth flow;
Free of their Oaths, but in performance slow.
Impunity renders the Traytors safe,
Even *Jove* at Lovers perjuries doth laugh.
Your Yielding Mind let not vain presents bend,
Beware of Gifts an Enemy doth send:
They are the price they'd buy You at, and when
You are their own, the Gifts are theirs again.
Be deaf to Flattery; it deludes the Mind,
And oft, when all Arts fail, doth entrance find.
But then's most Danger, we should to't resign,
When't meets with that *Arch-Flatterer* within.
Ne're dream, that *Constancy* in Man resides,
Who less i'th' Prize, then in the Conquest Prides,
In *Love* and in *Ambition* what Men have,
They slight, and for what they possess not, rave.
One Conquest got, another fills the Mind,
Nor can the greatest Treasures keep't confind.
Of Thoughts and of Desires no bounds are known,
Nor can the brightest Beauty fix Love down,
Nor will Preëminence more be You allow'd,
Once got, you're lost among the Common Crowd.
No greater Privilege will Your Beauty gain,
But in the Mass of things will Scorn'd remain,
Nor but for change be visited again.
The tasting *Bee* doth search the secret Bowers,
And rifles all the Beds of silver flowers:
Nor Rose, nor Lilly, can inforce his stay;
Fresh sweets the winged *Chymist* call away.
Untouch'd You'll th' object of their Worship be;
Yielding You do at their Discretion ly,
And when the Thief hath robb'd, he'll *hate* and *fly*.
See! The throat-parched *Wretch*, whom Thirst doth fire,
Approaches the cool Fount with hot desire. He

He bows his Head, and kneels upon the brink,
And freely o'th' transparent Waves doth drink.
Refresh'd, he careless doth pursue his way,
No thanks to th' charitable *Nymph* doth pay,
Nor her once-rav'shing Charms can beg his stay:
Rises and slights what he did late adore;
Turns his ungratefull Back, never to see her more.----

Thus sang my Friend--- But did Fair Martha *know*
The Truth *and Love, that in my Soul do flow;*
Her Virgin-Sweets She'd to my Arms resign,
Bless Me, *and bless Her Self in being Mine.*
No Goddess *e're deserv'd so well as She!*
And no True Lover *e're exceeded Me.*

The Twelve Rules of Friendship *to my Worthy Friend, M*r Joshua Barnes, B.D. *President of* Emmanuel *College in* Cambridge.

FRiendship's the purest, the Divinest Love,
The onely Passion, *Angels* know above:
Where purg'd from Matter Souls do truly join,
Abstracted from all sordid low design,
And where no Mixture of the *Sex* creeps in.
The *Gordian* Knot, that nothing can unty,
No Time can wear, nor date of Age destroy.
Whose Rules, without the gawdy Dress of Art,
Accept from Him, who freely sends his Heart.

FIRST RULE.

No Supercilious Look, no *Cato's* brow,
No surly State, or Pride, in *Friendship* show.

Act not a Maſter, or Superior's part
But freely to your *Friend* diſcloſe your Heart.
When *Friendſhip's* bonds concording Hearts do tie,
Why ſhould a diſtance 'twixt the Perſons lie?

II.

Be Deaf to Rumour, and to whiſper'd Lyes,
Which wicked Arts and Envious Tongues deviſe.
Detraction's ſecret-wounding Arrows fly
Silent as *Night*, and Black as *Deſtiny*.
Still keep *One* Ear for what your *Friend* may ſay:
Fame may deceive; in *Juſtice* Hear his Plea.

III.

No baſe, mean Action of your *Friend* deſire,
Nor baſely act for Him, if *He* require.
Do vertuouſly, you'll pleaſe your vertuous *Friend*,
If not, let *Friendſhip*, not your *Vertue*, end:
That *Friendſhip's* bad, which *Vertue* can't commend.

IV.

Warn him of Dangers, which he doth not ſee
Thrô *Ignorance*, or *Inadvertency*;
Chiefly thoſe Snakes, that under *Flowers* repoſe,
Pretended Friends, the very worſt of Foes:
From *theſe* our treacherous Diſappointments riſe;
Theſe know our Hearts, with *theſe* we do adviſe;
But Guard our ſelves from *Open Enemies*.

V.

Cauſleſs *Suſpicions* ſhun; they taint the Mind,
And make the beſt-meant Actions ſeem unkind.
Shew not too quick a ſenſe of Injuries,
Our greateſt Griefs do from Opinion riſe.
He, that on Trivial Grounds doth Frantick grow,
Doth live *Uneaſie*, and makes Friendſhip ſo.

VI. Ho

VI.

Honour your Friend's brave Acts with worthy Praise,
But don't your Eulogies to Flattery raise.
Labour'd Expressions flote above the Heart,
The Product not of Nature, but of Art.
Yet been't too sparing: If Extremes must be,
Let them upon the side of Kindness lie.

VII.

Severely Blame his faults, but Taunting spare.
Scorn from a Friend the deadli'est Sting doth wear,
And in a *Friend's* disguise a *Foe* is there.
Chide but with Goodness, blame with Clemency:
Publick Reproofs are kin to Calumny.
Comfort Him, if his Shame or Grief abound,
And pour in Oyl, when you have search'd the Wound.

VIII.

Speak well of Him; but shun officious Lies:
Immoderate Praises turn to Injuries.
Defend him Absent; Vindicate his Name,
And boldly from *Detraction* free his Fame.
Nay, if he's Justly taxt, excuse his Fault,
With all, from Truth, or Prudence, can be brought.

IX.

Be in your Kindness generous and free,
Give, but upbraid not: *That* turns Injury.
And when his Gratitude he'd make appear,
Accept his Presents, thô but mean they are.
Despise no Gift, that doth from Love proceed:
Slights and unkindness make Love deeply bleed.

X.

Counsel him Faithfully; let not Advice
From your Advantage or Designs arise.

We're all ill Judges of our Acts: Bless'd he,
Can with Impartial Eyes and Judgment see,
And hath a Friend, on whom he can rely.
His Interest be your Aim, and Truth your Guide:
Advise on Safety, not on Favour's side.

XI.

Be Gallant in's defence: For no design,
Fear, or unworthy thoughts your Love decline.
To' his Aid thrô strongest Opposition fly,
Nor draw your Hand back, till you've set him free.
Nothing's too dear for Friendship: For his sake
Your Name, Estate, and Life lay down at stake.

XII.

Value and prize his Kindness, Love him high,
In gallant Actions with his Friendship vie.
Wear him still next your Heart, the lasting stay,
When Health, Wealth, Pleasure, Honour fly away:
The mighty *Cordial*, that doth ease our trouble
Divides our Griefs, and makes our Pleasures double.

The Memorandum.

FRiendship can numerous *Mountain*-Faults pass by;
They are but Molehills in a Friendly Eye:
And *Love* can Multitudes of Sins conceal.---
But He, that *Secrets doth reveal*,
And what's entrusted to his Breast doth tell;
Or He, that treacherously his *Friend doth smite*,
Whispers Reproach, and stabs him in the Night,
Forfeits to all these Laws his Right:
Branded like *Cain*, like *Cain* accursed too,
Foe to the World, and all the World his Foe,
Never may He the Joys of sacred *Friendship* know!

On the Phænix.

I'M *Nature's* wonder, the Creation's glory,
Pride of *Arabia*, Prodigy of story:
On whom profusely Nature spends her store,
And after for a thousand years is Poor.
Wonder not then, she *Me* alone doth make;
So much from her my single Worth doth take,
Another cost would Bankrupt *Nature* break.
I, to my self both *Parent* am, and *Heir*;
My *Parent* Me, and I my *Parent* bear.
I'm always Diverse, and am yet the Same;
Find a new *Life* by *dying* in the Flame:
Chang'd, yet unchang'd, thrô endless Ages I
Wear out *alone* a long Eternity.
Nor yet can I with all my Pomp and State
Keep Scandal off, th' Attendant of the Great;
The *Sceptick* World only believes, I'm bred
In the warm Climes of a *Romantick* head.
My tedious Years I without Joys delude
In my uncomfortable Solitude:
The Birds and Beasts, and all the World besides
At Spring's approach do choose their Loving Brides,
Into Extatick Charms the hours improve,
And melt the Circling Moments into Love.
Those happy Minutes are to Me unknown,
Not all my Spices can their loss attone;
But I am curs'd, because I am Alone
" 'Tis oft the Lot o'th' eminently Great,
' To want those Pleasures, meaner Men await;
" *Captives* to Grandeur, and the *Slaves* of State.

An Epitaph on his Dear Friend Mr. Robert Cony, *the Younger, who died* November *the Ninth* 1681. *and lies buried in* Weypole-*Church in* Marchland Norf. *By* J. B.

IN Prime of Youth and near to Manhood drawn,
Here envious Night opprest my hopefull Dawn:
Before the Nuptial Crown adorn'd my Head;
Before I tasted of the Bridal Bed,
In Parent Dust seal'd up to Death I lie
A sad Example of Mortality.
Beauty and *Youth* and *Wit* and *Wealth* are vain;
For I had *All*: Yet all could not obtain
A short Reprieve from the Unwelcome Grave:
The last Possession, that Poor Man must have.
Then let All know, how Nought by Death's regarded;
And *Vertue's* in the other World rewarded.

To my Worthy Friend Mr. Joshua Barnes B D. *Senior Fellow of* Emmanuel *College, on his Incomparable History of King* EDWARD *the* Third, *&c.*

TO bring back *Fate*, which knows not to Return;
And raise the *Heroes* from their silent Urn;

Long-

Long-paſt revolving Ages to reſtore,
And Acts, done many hundred Years before,
Mauger Oblivion, in Juſt Garbs to dreſs,
And bring Auguſt *Shades* from their dark Receſs,
Out of the gloomy hidden Cave; where ly
Days paſt, like Dreams, and waning Moons fled by;
And mixed Heaps of loſt Mortality:
To raiſe the World anew; loſt Years to trace,
Make preſent Times to Ages paſt give place;
And Monarchs once again with their old Crowns to Grace:
Fame's quite-ſpent Lamp more brightly to Renew:-----
Seem'd, Learned *Friend*, a Task befitting *You.*

The Ancients dream'd of Charmes, that brought the Moon
From her bright Orb, ſtrugling, enraged, down:
But None could e're dark *Shades* to Life reſtore,
And break Fate's Adamantine Gates before;
Except *Alcides* and *Apollo's* * Son;
This *They* could do, and *You* as much have done:
Nay more, for *You* no common Life do give;
Your Heroes to Eternity do Live!
With this Addition to their ſmiling Fate,
You make them Happy, as You make them Great,
And add not onely to their *Life*, but *State.*
Old *Time* in Your Learn'd Work grows *Young* again:
In You our Valiant *Worthies* Live and Reign.
Their Souls, as Rivers under Mountains Dive
And after in the open Air revive,
In our Great WILLIAM and his Captains Live.
The Mighty *Grafton* like Your *Chandos* fell,
He liv'd, as *Bravely*, and He dy'd, as well:
To *Edward* That, and This to *William* Dear,
And both the GARTER'S honour'd Badge did wear:
Both dy'd too ſoon:--But both Immortal are.

* *Æſculapius.*

Nor

Nor do Your *Heroes* now Ignobly stand;
Once more they Influence their Native Land:
You give them Life, and they do Souls bestow,
They actuate the Sencelefs Clods below;
Reading their Acts Cowards do Valiant grow.
Th' Effeminate Gallant, on his Bed of Ease,
Feels a new Warmth on all his Vitals seize;
Gets a new Soul from each enlivening Word,
Rises a Champion, and calls for his Sword.
Nothing to' exalt our Glory doth remain,
But to Read *You*, and grow True *Englishmen*:
Your *Book* alone would armed Troops advance,
To claim once more our *long-lost Right* to FRANCE.

How Boundlefs was Your Mind; to fill that Sphear,
Where sparkling *Fame* did lofty Trophies rear!
How Fair and Beauteous Your Idæas were!
That could the Treaties, Councels, Battels, show;
Stupendious Acts, that made even Fate to bow;
And but seem'd fit for Your BLACK-PRINCE to do,
That Reign of Wonder; Gem of Times; the Glory,
But hardest part, of all the *English* Story:
When one Sun by our Conquering Arms beheld,
Two Monarchs slain, a Third to quit the Field;
Two Captive Kings to *London*'s Tower were brought,
And injur'd Princes here for Comfort sought.
Our *Edward* then, the whole World's Love and Fear,
Did at his Will the Fate of Kingdoms steer:
Held *Europe*'s Ballance, and fix'd *Fortune's* Wheel,
And where he turn'd, made Fate's strong Pillars reel.
To *Merit* more, than to *Possess*, did choose;
And proffer'd *Empire* bravely did refuse.
When, Honour's Darling, his Victorious SON,
Kings, as He pleas'd, could make, or could dethrone:
And all the Neighbouring Monarchs thought their Crowns,
Fix'd with his *Smiles*, but tottering with his *Frowns*. When

When *England* was the Theatre of Fame,
And Warriours hither to gain Honour came.
Our EDWARD solely *Valour's* Umpire stood,
His Approbation made the *Brave* and *Good.*
Then High Exploits, and Acts on Vertue plac'd,
Above *French* Princes *English* Commons rais'd:
That *Subjects* (*Vertue* makes the meanest Great)
Five Kings at once could at their Tables treat.
When Victory due to Piety was given:
Their *Arms* forc'd Kingdoms and their *Prayers* took Heaven.
When *Valiant* and *Religious* Acts could meet,
Christian and *Souldier* mutually did greet.
History before was but like *Fairy* Land,
That thick with Monsters and wild Shapes did stand:
'Twas modell'd, not to' instruct; but cheat the Mind,
Truth and its usefull Ends were left behind,
And all for Flattery and mean Arts design'd.
But You did all its Primitive Worth restore;
Truth never look'd so Beautifull before.
Above Expression Soars the lofty Mind;
But You fit *Words* do for great *Actions* find.
Your lofty *Style's* fill'd with such Manly Heat;
You could have *fought* the Battels, that You *writ.*
Bold and Expressive, fit for Godlike Men:
Mars tun'd Your Soul and *Phœbus* steer'd Your Pen.
Our Souls go, as we read; our Present State,
Is lost i'th' Mighty Acts, that You relate;
We Joy at Good and Grieve at Adverse Fate.
We Glorious Patterns in each Line do read,
And here we truly may *consult the Dead.*
And now—— —— ——
You, Modern Sparks, that in degenerate *Ease,*
Or active *Vice* spend Your ignoble Days!

That ne're did crown'd with Forreign Trophies come,
But brought the Vices and Diseases home:
Senceless of-Fame to late Posterity,
You can't be mention'd but for Infamy,
While Your great Sires embalm'd in Honour ly.
Read This---and blush to see, how You disgrace
Those Names, whom *Vertue* to the Stars did raise,
Your *Ancestors*, their own and Nation's Fame,
You, their Degenerate Sons, to Both a Shame.
They Conquer'd *France*, which now Your Arms outbraves;
You're Apes to those, were Your Forefathers Slaves.
  Why then, my Friend, should Your bright Rays be hid?
And You, that can new Life bestow, ly Dead?
Show to the World, You are for all things fit,
In *History* True, in * *Poetry* a Wit.
That Your *Black-Prince* can now in *You* acquire
What *Alexander* did in vain desire,
An *Homer*, who his Godlike Acts might praise,
And sound his Honour forth in endless Layes.
So sung by You, shall *CRESSY*'s deathless Field,
Neither to *Homer's* Pen, nor *Maro's* yield.
But th' *English* Valour then shall soar as high,
As ever well-tongu'd *Greece* or *Rome* could fly.
Then Kings shall bribe Your Verse, and each Crown'd Head
With emulous Strife shall beg Your *Muse's* Aid:
Shall doe Great Acts, to be rehears'd by *You*;
And *Vertue* for *Your Praise's* sake pursue.
The Greatest Monarchs court You for their Friend,
And *Presents*, to bespeak your *Favour*, send:
Jealously strive each other to outvie
In Gifts to *You*; Who can return them *Immortality*.

* *Poema* Latinum *Heroicum* Franciados *dictum Libb.* 12. *jamjam absolvendum.*

On

On Old Age.

I.

OLD-*Age*, the State we all desire,
For none would immaturely die:
But Riddles in our Nature lie;
Thô we with frequent Prayers do it require;
Yet when Indulgent Heaven grants our Request,
How are we with its Weight opprest?

II.

In vain we for *Content* do seek;
Tir'd with what doth to us betide,
We wish for things as yet untri'd,
Which, when we have obtain'd, we still dislike.
Gray hairs we pray for, yet when they are come,
We querulously curse our Doom.

III.

So *Life* we do accept, and yet,
If we beforehand could foresee
Of our few days the Misery,
And had our choice, All would refuse the Cheat.
At all Adventures it becomes our Lot,
And's given to those, that know it not.

IV.

Except we early Victims fall,
Yet we this *State* must undergo:
When *Age* shall wrinkle *Cælia*'s brow,
When *Milo* shall his shrunken Limbs bewail:
When all the Joys, do upon Youth attend,
Shall in unwelcome Aches end.

V.

Yet 'tis our fault, this State don't please;
Our *Youth* we foolishly engage,
And no Provision make for *Age.*
Inherent Vanity our Mind doth seize;
None of those Vertues laid in store, that might
Give to the wearied Mind delight.

VI.

The Wise and Vertuous well the Time can spend
When the disinterested Mind
None of the Body's fetters bind;
But Peace and Fame do on Gray hairs attend:
When well-spent Days add to the Aged powers,
And to Old Years insert Young hours.

VII.

The cooler hours of elder Days
Are well adapted to Delight,
On whom no turbulent Passions light:
'Tis folly that doth every state debase.
" Nothing more monstrous to the World appears,
" Than *Gray-hair'd Fools*, or *Children of old Years.*

Plutarch's *Serpent.*

A Subtle Serpent, that long time did reign
O're all the Subjects of the spacious Plain;
That often to old Age did Youth afford
And with his cast-off Skin new strength restor'd;
In his Divided bosome long did bear
The fatal seeds of an Intestine war.
Th' Ambitious *Tail*, that long time had been led
(And Justly too) by Conduct of the *Head*;

To *Jove* complain'd, that now it was but due,
That he should Govern for a Day or two.
In anger *Jove* did to the prayer consent
To teach Ambitious Fools to be content;
And a Decree unalterable made,
That in no case the *Head* should lend his Aid.
The *Tail*, a part of great Activity,
But with a curse annext, *It cannot see*,
With haughty Pride assumes the fatal state,
And makes the once-commanding *Head* to wait:
What was his Lord doth in proud Triumph draw,
And now despises what once gave the Law.
Proud of the Government thrô Woods he hies,
O're Rocks and fatal Precipices flies.
The Head beholds the Danger and doth fear,
The stupid *Tail* hath neither Eye, nor Ear;
Nor Reason to perceive, when Danger's near.
Till, after many dreadfull Perils past,
The wrigling *Tail* in narrow holes at last,
And dark blind Caverns, is past help set fast.
Forward he cannot, backward must not move,
And no way's left, but to Petition *Jove*.
Jove is implor'd, but's Deaf unto the cry,
In the deserved plague doth let him die;
And to the World doth a sad warning shew,
" *What*, when the *Rabble* governs, *will ensue*.

The Looking-Glass to Gellia.

FOR Interest Men know how to please,
And praise even your Deformities:
Wither'd and Old you shall be Young,
And purchase Beauty from their Tongue,

Not

Not your own Art their Wit shall want,
They'l doe in Words, what you in Paint.
If You do laugh, why † I laugh too;
If You do weep, to weep I know:
Yet think not, 'tis for flattery meant;
I what You are do represent.
When You was Young, I show'd You so,
And alter, now You alter, too:
Yet thó I thus Extreams do try,
The Change in You not Me doth lie.
When You with Paint bedaub your Face;
And call back long-lost Youthfull Grace:
When You new Sets of *Teeth* prepare;
And deck your *Head* with others Hair:
When You your hated *Breath* perfume,
And line your *Mouth*, that stinks of Rheume:
'Tis not my fault, that You look Fair;
I truly show the Cheats, You wear.
With Shows You first the World deceive,
I back to You the Poison give.
Yet, faithless *Gellia*, know among
The Arts you have to make You Young,
Death can't be chouc'd with borrow'd Grace,
Nor will mistake your Painted Face.
Not all your Instruments of Pride
Your Age's Date from him can hide.
Death knows his Time, will surely come,
And lay You *old* and *ugly* in your Tomb.

On Speech.

I.

THOU wondrous Modulation of the Air,
The brightest *Index* of the Heart:
Who all those Lively Signatures dost bear,
By which our thoughts to others We impart!

What elſe would in Oblivion's ſhadows ſleep,
To Knowledge by thy help doth creep!

II.

There's not a ſecret paſſion of the Mind,
No Motion in the Soul doth riſe;
But it from *Speech* can fit Expreſſions find,
And's Judged of more by the Ears, than Eyes.
How do fit Words and Sentences advance,
And on our Tongues in order dance!

III.

In various ſounds the ſenceleſs Creatures play,
And welcome the returning Spring:
Their joys i'th' rudeſt notes the *Beaſts* Eſſay;
And tunefull *Birds* their warbling Carols ſing,
Diſtinct their Voices; only *Man* is found;
That can *Artitulate the Sound.*

IV.

Admired *Faculty*, that ſtamps the Air,
And ſeals upon't, what We would have,
Which doth a Draught of our *Ideas* bear,
And keeps the ſpeaking Portraitures, We gave,
Doth the Myſterious tract of Thoughts unfold;
Thô each Tongue hath a different Mold!

V.

This Privilege, granted alone to *Man*,
No other Creatures do partake:
Beaſts have no Language, 'tis well known; nor can
We prove, what Speech *Angels* above do ſpeak.
All that belongs to them do Myſteries grow,
Stupendious heights, we never know.

VI.

Angelick Motions we can never find,
Nor trace the ſteps, in which they move,
To our Infirmities they'r not confin'd,
Nor Nature's Laws do fetter them above.

All, that we know of those Superiour Powers
Is, that their State is not like Ours.

VII.

They may by Heavenly *Hieroglyphicks* speak,
To which our Souls can never rise:
Draughts of their thoughts by forms or figures make,
Or unintelligible Mysteries.
Their Tongue all apprehension doth excell,
No Ear can hear't, no Voice can tell.

VIII.

What empty shrunken things our Minds would be,
What Melancholy on them seize;
Were they debarr'd the Joys of Phantasie,
And roving Thoughts, which the tir'd Soul do ease:
Where in unbounded fields the Mind may fly,
And find new blandishments for Joy.

IX.

How much more miserable were our State,
Were This, our greatest Comfort, fled;
That mollifies the Stings of angry Fate;
Unloads the Sorrows of the anxious Head:
Doth cure the Wounds, that from *Fate's* Arrows fall,
And in a *Friend's* Breast buries all:

X.

Delight of Life and Mirrour of the Heart,
By which our Thoughts, which none can see,
We to our own and others Joys impart;
And bring to View the boundless Treasury.
Thou of our Inward Soul a Scheme should'st give; ---
And curs'd be He, that doth *Deceive*!

XI.

Bond of Society and Tie of Love,
From whence doth lasting Friendship flow:
Thou our Exalted pleasure dost improve;
And art the Universal Soul below.

With

With raptur'd Joys thou charm'st the fleeting Hours,
And lull'st up Love in shady Bowers.

XII.

Rhetorick, that doth th' unstable People move
And raise, or lay, as Storms the Sea,
From well-plac'd Words and Reasons doth improve,
And ows his Energy, bless'd *Speech*, to Thee.
What was a *Chaos*, thou a World did'st make;
From thee the Mass did Beauty take.

XIII.

The Raptur'd Flights of *Poetry* do owe
Their Birth and Beauty unto Thee:
From Thee the fam'd *Castalian* Waters flow,
And in soft Musick's Numbers melted bee.
How low would all their Lofty Flights be laid,
If not in Robes by Thee array'd?

XIV.

Reason may in the solid Mind be found,
And Judgment in the Soul appear:
But they'r like Treasures buried under ground,
Or secret Mines, that do no Products bear.
Thou deck'st them in Rich Garbs, and mak'st them shine;
Thou stamp'st them, and they'r currant Coin.

On Time.

THou saw'st (and oh! how glorious was the sight?)
When the Creation smil'd at Infant Light,
And banish'd all the Dismall shades of Night.
When the bright Births at fruitfull Heaven's command
Immac'ulate drop'd from the Great *Workman's* hand,
E're Sin, or Curse, their genuine Beauty stain'd.

The Rowling Ages, that have since slid by,
Have all been brought forth by thy Midwifry:
From the first Monarch, but without a Crown,
To *Him*, that last forsook th' Uneasie Throne.
Thou saw'st at first, when swelling Families,
(Widely dispersing round their Colonies)
Did into Towns; Towns into Cities rise.
When Right of Empire was in *Fatherhood*,
And every one was King of his own Blood.
Till the Paternal Rule in Numbers lost,
In various Multitudes and Errours crost,
The Reins of Empire were by *One* ingrost.
Thou saw'st the Faults, in the first Empire grew,
The vicious Habits, its Destruction drew:
Till th' fatal Period swiftly hurrying on,
The mighty *Babel* from its height was thrown,
And from its shatter'd Limbs, in pieces broke,
Their Rise the lesser States and Kingdoms took:
Till one above the rest more Powerfull grown,
For *Justice*, *Valour*, and for *Wisedom* known,
Exalts by secret steps her lofty head,
And, some by *kindness* won, and some by *dread*,
O're all at last doth her wide Empire spread.
Till she, or *Cruel*, or *Effeminate* grown,
Less hurt by others Arms, than by her own,
Falls into th' Pit of sure Destruction.

Thus hast thou view'd the slippery State of things,
The *Persian*, *Grecian*, and the *Roman* Kings:
And shortly shal't the sad *Catastrophe*
And Fall o'th' now-decreasing *CRESCENT* see.

Wisest of Beings! What we do design,
And in dark Caverns of our Breast confine;
Ev'n where no *Thought* comes, where no *Eye* can peep,
But all's lap'd up in misty Clouds of sleep,

What

What Princes wish, or Cabinet Councils plot,
The Births, that are from their Conjunction got,
Subtlest *Interpreter*, thou dost reveal;
Thô Oaths and Sanctions do the secret Seal.
Even what Just Heaven before the World decreed,
What can from nothing, but his Hand proceed:
What shall to Peasants happen, what to Kings,
What to the Lofty, what to Humbler things:
What swallows up Man's bold and daring Mind,
And where even *Angels* can no footsteps find:
What doth surpass th' Intelligences sight,
Or *hath*, or *shall* by Thee be brought to Light.
Nor is't enough, thou saw'st the former days,
And in our Times know'st, what will come to pass:
But when this Generation hath its Doom,
And crowding Numbers in our Places come;
When all, that now is High, must Low be laid,
And Generations after Us are dead:
Then Thou wilt see, what now doth fly our Eyes,
What Abject People shall to Empire rise:
Where Mighty Citties, now their Nation's Glory,
Shall lie in Dust and be forgot in Story:
And in some unthought unsuspected place,
Others shall in their Room their proud Heads raise.
What Families shall up to Rule be born,
Whom Ages past ne're knew, or else did scorn:
And all be to such Alteration brought,
The very Ancient Names of things forgot:
That even the World may in the World be sought.
The Mighty Innovator *Time*, that brings
Those changes, are not in the Power of Kings.
What neither their Commands nor Arms can raise,
By secret unknown means He brings to pass.

Should *Scipio* or should *Cæsar* now awake,
And into Light from their dark Mansions break;
Should They, to what was the World's *Mistress*, come,
How would they wonder at once Glorious *Rome*!
Their once-known Palaces would seek in vain,
Nor their Triumphal Arches find remain:
But She that did of the World's Empire boast,
See in her Heaps of Scatter'd Ruines lost;
And to such steps of Desolation led
Her very Name and Valour buried.
Little they thought, what Time would once bring forth,
That the despised People of the *North*,
The Barbarous Scum, which *Roman* Souls did hate,
The Dregs and Lees of Men and Scourge of Fate,
Should thrô the Barrs of that strong Empire break,
And the vast Fabrick into pieces shake,
That other Nations proud with their Success,
Should their own Fame and *Rome*'s Contempt increase:
Till o're Her every Land did Conquest boast,
And took again what their Forefathers lost.
They knew not what was in *Fate's* leaves enrol'd,
Nor would have credited, had they been told:
Such Revolutions there's no Art can tell;
'Tis only *Time*, that will the Truth reveal.
Time! Thou dost bring things into open view,
But Thou can'st drink a Cup of *Lethe* too.
Thou over all dost draw a sullen Cloud,
And dost in Mists, what's now apparent shrow'd;
The Acts of Ancient Days, to us unknown,
Buried long since in deep Oblivion:
What *Heroes* did, and Common People bore,
Forgetfull *Time*, thou can'st not now restore!
Those Noble Seats, that Honour'd once our Isle,
When *Roman* Eagles nested in our Soil,

How

Low with their Mistress *Rome* in dust are laid;
No footstep's found, may lead unto their Head:
Are sought in vain among their poor remains,
Shown but to puzzle Antiquaries Brains.
As Father Ocean *here to Earth doth Lend,*
And there his Watry Empire doth extend;
So thou dost sometimes new Inventions show,
But hidest other Rarer Matters low.
Tobacco, Guns, *and* Printing *late arose,*
But We are Rob'd of Richer things, than those;
Faith, Justice, Honour, Liberality,
And Ancient Friendship *deep in* Lethe *ly.*
Where is an Hero *now, that owns a* Muse?
Hawks, Hounds, *and* Mistresses *they'd rather choose.*
Thy Essence doth a Train of Wonders hold:
Thou never art above a Moment old,
Yet Thou beheld'st the rude misshapen Mass,
E're *Light*, Heaven's First-born, show'd her darling Face.
The Circling Years do dy and leave their Place,
And new Times in their rooms their Heads do raise:
Yet Thou Coæval with the World dost Live,
And to its utmost Period shalt survive.
Thou'rt ever here, and yet art ever past,
Thou'rt ever dying, yet dost ever last.
Thy subtle Parts always in Motion be,
Yet Thou dost ever a Succession see.
Waves crowd on Waves, and while We look they'r past,
And Eager Brethren after them do hast.
These press the former, those behind them press,
Nor let the fresh Supplies the Stream decrease:
New Waves the Place of what pass'd by retain;
The River yet unchanged doth remain.
Thou of all Jewels the most Precious, (*Time*!)
Of all the Stores o'th' *East* or *Western* Clime.

Impe-

Imperious Gold, that all things doth command,
Whose powerfull Charms there's nothing can withstand;
Doth here an End of his vast Empire see;
That cannot have an Influence over Thee.
Thy moving Wheels cannot be stop'd by force,
No Bribes perswade Thee to renew thy Course:
Deaf to Intreaties, and to all our Moan,
"Once past, Thou'rt lost, and art for ever gone.
A *Drug*, while Thou upon our hand dost stay,
Which We well know not how to throw away:
But when thou'rt past, a *Jewel* in our Eye;
Whom not the Treasures of the World can buy.
Ages before our Birth We can't recall;
They no Relation have to Us at all:
What then was done, as We can ne're retrieve,
So neither are We bound account to give.
The Future Time We know not, that 'twill come;
We may before to morrow have our Doom;
We may be Summon'd by Death's Mighty Power:
And when We dy, *Time* is to Us no more.
"The Present *Time's* then all the Time We have,
"Those precious Moments our best Conduct crave:
"That We be Wise our latest Stake to Save.

On a Covetous *Man.* Mart. Lib.4.Ep.40.

WHen Heaven to You a small Estate did lend,
You kept your Coach and Footmen did attend:
But when blind *Fortune* had your Store increas'd,
And ten times doubled what You had at least:
Your Narrow Soul, contracted with the Store,
Lost all the Pleasure, it did tast before.

A Curse into your Treasures Heaven did put;
You groan'd beneath their weight, and went afoot.
For all your Merits what doth then remain;
But that we pray, Heaven send your Coach again?

Dorinda *weeping.*

I.

STAY pretty Prodigal, oh stay;
Throw not those Pearly Drops away:
Each little shining Gem might be
Price for a Captive Prince's Liberty.
See down her Cheeks the shining Jewels slide,
Brighter than Meteors, that from Heaven do glide.

II.

Sorrow ne're look'd before so Fair,
Nor ever had so sweet an Air:
All-conquering Rays her Woes do dart,
And unknown Passions to the Soul impart.
More Fair she looks, while *Grief* her face doth shrowd;
Than the *Sun* peeping thrô a *watry* cloud.

III.

Oh turn away those Killing Eyes! ---
Venus from such a Sea did rise.
Love doth in Tears triumphant ride;
Such mighty Charms can never be deni'd:
That at one sight such different Passions move,
Relenting *Pitty* and Commanding *Love*.

IV.

Come, curious *Artist*, as they fall,
Gather the shining Jewels all:
Harden the Gems, and each will be
More valued, than the *Indie's* Treasury;

But if the secret doth exceed thy Art,
It is but borrowing *Hardness* from her *Heart*.

To Sr. James Butler, *on the Death of the Lady* Butler: *In a Dialogue between* H. *and* J.

(*H.*) WElcome dear *Friend*! Thou dost my Griefs dispell,
No Sorrow long can wound, when Thou art well.
Ill-boding Dreams o're my sad Fancy rowl'd,
And the approach of some black Fate foretold:
Strange frightfull Spectres o're my Mind were spread;
I saw the Vertues and the Graces bleed,
As thô the Soul o'th' Universe was dead.
Avert the *Omen* Heaven!
(*J.*) Thy Cautions spare,
There's nothing left that now deserves thy Care.
All Worth and Excellence with *One* is fled,
The Quintessence of all, that's Great, is dead.
Th' Expiring World groan'd at Her Funeral,
With whom the Glories of her *Sex* did fall.
(*H.*) What ill do my Presaging thoughts Divine?
Spare One, Just Heaven, I'll to thy Will resign;
One Inno'cent spare; and all the rest be Thine.
(*J.*) We multiply the sorrows, that we dread, ---
Meet then the Storm that hover's o're thy Head;
The Fair, Chaste, Spouse of Noble *Butler's* dead.
(*H*) Too much---Fate hath not now a Curse in store,
I've heard the worst of Ills, and Fear no more.
(*J.*) The whole World seem'd *distracted* at her fall,
Amazing *Horrour* seized upon All.

So

So, when the *Sun's* Eclips'd, with *Panick* fear
The Savages confused Cries do rear,
And think, the World's *Catastrophe* is near.
With frightfull Fury hideously they roar
To scare the Monster, would the *Sun* devour.
They gain their Point, but we lament in vain,
Our *Sun* is set, [illegible] to Rise again.
(*H.*) Yet let's Lament; 'tis all that we can doe,
To think of Bliss, that's past, amidst our Wo,
Heightens *our Grief*; *but* vents *our Sorrows too.*
(*J.*) She fell an Holocaust of Chast Delight,
Beauteous and Fair, as Rays of new-born Light.
Charming, as *Vertues* i'th' *Idea* be,
Or *Graces*, seen by th' *Intellectual* Eye.
(*H.*) So falls the *Rose*, Queen of the fragrant Bowers,
She falls the Glory o'th' Enamell'd Flowers,
While Heav'en laments her Death in melting Showers.
(*J.*) To blooming *Youth* a boundless *Wit* was given,
Not got with Labour, but infus'd from Heaven.
Beauty did o're her Soul and Body shine,
Her Body seem'd, ev'n as her Soul, *Divine.*

CHORUS.

Wit, Youth, *and* Beauty *made Her Bright,*
Did all in Her agree:
None else, but Phœbus, *God of Light,*
Is Sourse of all the Three.

(*H.*) *Angels* can't sin: They'r plac'd in such a State,
They nor can Fall, nor can Degenerate.
They merit Praise, who by their Choice are Good,
Not those, who can't be Vitious, if They wou'd.
Nor justly can Rewards to *Angels* come;
Vertue's not Abstinence in them, but Doom.

How high and Glorious do Her acts appear,
That liv'd in Heaven, thô in this lower Sphear:
And, thô a Mortal, rival'd *Angels* here?
They've no Temptation, and She scorned all:
They live Above, She trampled on this *Ball.*
To what was Good, like *Angels*, vigorous still,
And every thing did Dare to doe, but Ill.
(*F.*) What *Vertues* were there, but her Soul did grace,
Vertues not known, but in an Higher place,
Nor acted, but by the *Seraphick* Race?
Her Help, like Guardian *Angels*, she bestow'd,
Bounteous as Nature, or as Nature's God.
On all she look'd with an *Auspicious* Ray,
So Good, from Her none went displeas'd away.
And so Devout, she seem'd all o'r Divine,
That *Hallelujah's* her whole task had been,
Or that one Saint pray'd at another's *Shrine.*
(*H.*) She's Dead! not all her Worth could bribe her Fate;
So in the Grave, divested of all state,
Lie Young and Old, the Humble and the Great.
Thou, *Butler's* Hero, who 'mong all the Stars
Of Courtly Beauties ne're saw'st One like Hers,
Art left like Us in vain to seek relief:
" Greatness is not exempt from Fate or Grief.
That Loss is trivial, which we can supply,
How stinging that, which Riches cannot buy,
Nor doth i'th' reach of Art or Honour lie!
To Thee a while the Heavenly Form was show'd,
Worthy the Gift or Ransome of a God.
Thy blessed Arms the Treasure did enfold,
(Too soon, alass! with Saints to be enrold.)
And when thy Soul did to high Transports rise,
She sunk from thy Admiring, Longing, Eyes.

Who

Who can wish Thee thy Sorrows to refrain?
Even the Souls in Hell know no such Pain,
As once to' *have been in Heaven* and then *to lose't again.*
(*J.*) Farewell, Heaven's *Best of Gifts*! In *Thee* were laid
Perfections, that have Gods of Mortals made.
Greatness of Soul, without insulting *Pride.*
Humility, where no mean thoughts reside;
And *Vertue*, unto *Candour* near ally'd!
(*H.*) Thou *Highest* Point, that *Nature* could attain,
The *Moddel*, She can never reach again.
Th' *Acme*, to which our finite Worth can rise,
Perfect, if Ought can be below the Skies.

CHORUS.

The World no longer gives us Ease,
All here must loathsome be:
But doubly Heaven *our Souls will please,*
When there *We meet with* Thee.

On a Pearl.

I.

THE daring *Negro* dives for Me,
And I'm the noble Price of Blood:
Blind with my Rays he doth no danger see.
The common Stones in Quiet sleep,
Nor are torn from their Mother's Arms, the Deep.
So curs'd 'tis to be eminently Good;
No Rocks, nor shelters Me can shrowd.

II.

Some say, I am condensed Dew,
And from high Heaven my Extract claim:
That Drops, whom Night upon the Sea doth strow,

My eager Parents swallow down,
Till they are big with Heavenly *Embrio's* grown:
From Pearly Drops of Dew at first I came,
And hardned I am but the same.

III.

My Worth I from *Opinion* get,
And roving thoughts o'th' empty Mind:
In Me the Price of Provinces to eat,
The lavish *Cleopatra* taught,
And drink dissolved Kingdoms at a Draught.
Such Sparkling Juice not Gods themselves can find;
But must to *Nectar* be confin'd.

IV.

Condens'd in Regions of the Main,
The Wise think Me a Sunbeam set;
Where I my *Orient* hew unchang'd retain:
When *Sol* doth gild fair *Thetis* face,
And the Sea represents a Burning-glass;
Where the contracted Rays in one do meet,
Hardned by Cold they Me beget.

V.

Yet thô I'm of Æthereal kind,
My Habitation is but mean;
To rugged Rocks and Oyster-shells confin'd:
So Heaven doth many a Gallant Mind,
To a deformed crazy Body bind.
Both promise little, while the Shell is seen,
But yet the *Pearl* is found within.

On the Earth, *our Common Mother.*

THOU Universal *Mother* of Us all,
From whom the Creatures have Original;

From

From Monarch *Man*, with awfull Empire crown'd,
To the base *Reptile* creeping on the ground.
There's nothing, that hath Life, but owes its Birth
To Father *Sun* and teeming Mother *Earth*.
With genial Warmth *He* doth Her bosom heat,
She with wide Arms doth his Embraces meet:
Conceives, grows big, and from Her fruitfull Womb,
The Lovely Births in Beauteous Order come.
Nor Life alone Her Liberal Hand doth give,
Her Bosom bears the Food, on which they Live.
With needfull Herbage She doth cloath the Field,
That Nourishment to Man and Beast doth yeild.
Each Species of Her Creatures finds Her Good,
Appropriating to each kind Her Food.
And, that the Generations might not end,
With seminal Vertue She doth them befriend.
Each Creature gets his Like, and not one Plant
A way to Propagate his Kind doth want.
Unlike the Tree, from whence it fell, the Seed
By wondrous Vertue doth the Species breed.
And, what no form o'th' Parent doth retain,
By *Plastick* Power doth get its Like again.
Nor is She Mother and kind Nurse alone;
Her Arms receive Us, when our Race is run:
And when our wearied Days we bring to end,
We find Her Bosom an Eternal Friend.
There in our Resting-place we all lie down,
All sence of Grief and former Sorrow flown,
" Life is to Trouble ty'd, the Grave to none.
The former Ages, that long since slid by,
At Quiet in Her Clasping Arms do ly.
The *King* and *Peasant* do together rest:
No Pride fills One, nor Envy th' Other's breast.
The present Ages the same Fate shall have,
Tend to their Common Resting-place the Grave.

And

And Ages not yet sprung from Fate's Decree,
When they've run out the Line of Destiny,
(An equal Fate Death upon all things brings)
Shall all be lost i'th' Mass and crowd of Things.
So doth the River borrow from the Main
Those Streams, that rest not, till they'r there again.
From its first Rise thrô devious ways it goes,
With swift unwearied Course to th' Sea it flows,
And in its Mother's Lap seeks long Repose.

The Parting Lover.

I.

BEneath a Mournfull *Yew*, more than half-Dead,
The Melancholy *Damon* sate;
With Moving Accents sighing out his Fate,
The Object of his Passion fled:
Cælia, the Glory of the Plains,
Cælia, the Flame of all the Youthfull Swains;---
With pale dead Eyes he saw her Flight,
His Eyes Just closing in Eternal Night.
His loaden bosom thus his Sorrow spoke,
His Words and Heart thus at one instant broke.

II.

" So by Design or Chance, some Lonely Wretch,
" Left on a distant, *Northern*, Land
" With Swelling Eyes beholds the barren Strand,
" Th' uncomfortable, naked, Beach;
" Where grizely *Famine* leads the way,
" Fruitfull in nothing, but in Beasts of Prey.
" Monsters behind his back do roar,
" The Sea Destruction doth present before.
" And if to Heaven he looks with weeping Eyes,
" He sees that setting Sun, that ne're will rise.

III. " What

III.

" What shall He do, lost Wretch! Where shall He go?
" His Sighs the Fatal Winds increase;
" And flouds of Tears do swell the Mounting Seas:
" All things conspire unto his Woe.
" The ragged Rocks no comfort give,
" The barren Sands on them forbid to Live.
" With sooty Wings sad Night draws on,
" A Night, that ne're will see a Rising Sun:
" Till griping *Famine* him doth eat away,
" Or He to hungry Jaws becomes a Prey.

IV.

" And to increase his Woe, far off at Sea
" The Ship, in which his Hope's confin'd,
" Opens Her Bosom to the Prosperous Wind,
" Regardless of his Misery.
" Loudly He doth of Fate complain,
" Loudly laments his Wretched State in vain.
" The Noisy Billows cannot hear;
" Relentless Rocks are deaf unto his Prayer,
" The floating Ships before the Winds do play:
" The Winds bear them, his Hopes, and fruitless Prayers away.

The Chase of the Fox at *Welby* 1677. *To* St. John Bennet of *Welby*, Esquire.

THE Morn was fair and still; the Heaven was clear,
And not one sullen Star would disappear:
The Winds were not yet up; but in their Beds
In a deep Sleep had sunk their Drowsie Heads:
The Sluggard *Sun* had not yet left his Rest,
Nor rais'd his weary Head from *Thetis* Breast:
When I in Field a Gallant Train did meet,
For Vigorous Sport and Generous Actions fit:

They

They all on winged Coursers mounted stay
And big with Expectation wait the *Prey.*
Their curious Spies they first send out to try
And make Discovery of the Enemy:
These scorn, as others do, to trust the *Sight,*
Abus'd so oft, so seldom in the Right:
Which every palpable Appearance scapes,
And cheats it with Imaginary shapes:
A surer Guide leads these sagacious Spies,
That makes the *Nose* supply the place of *Eyes.*
Their cautious Foe, the *Fox,* had fled the Light,
And wisely before Day had *crept* from sight;
Gorg'd with his Prey, and in his Brakes immur'd,
Fearless He slept and thought himself secur'd:
But his Pursuers trace his hidden Course,
And follow him by a *Magnetick* Force,
First they employ their curious *Nose* to find
Those subtle *Atoms,* he had left behind:
Those Exhalations in his Footsteps lie,
That from his Breath, or from his Sweat do flie;
So small, they to our Eyes do disappear,
And undiscern'd mix with the Common Air.
These, as i'th' wanton Wind they play about,
Their Noses, *Chymist*-like, can draw them out;
And following the Stream, these Atoms make,
Run to the place, from whence the Fountain brake.
Mean while the *Fox,* wak'd with th' unusual Noise,
And with Attentive Ears catching the Voice,
Fears some Pursuers; but doth wonder, how
Thrô all his Mazes they his Course should know:
What Eyes could trace his Footsteps on the Green,
What Witchcraft thus could follow him unseen,
But now not trusting to a Longer stay
Resolves with silent Steps to steal away,

And uſe thoſe ſecret Arts, and that Deceit,
With which his raging Followers he could cheat:
But as he thrô the ſhady *Goſs* doth ſlide,
By one o'th' Watchfull Huntſmen he's eſpi'd.
His Joyfull Horn doth quickly tell it out,
And's Eccho'd back again by all the Rout:
A noiſe more Diſmall than the *Mandrake's* Voice,
A Noiſe, that chills the *Fox's* Blood to Ice.
The Sentence not more ſad to th' Guilty Man,
Or Cannon to the trembling *Indian*.
Thunder ſpeaks Muſick to't. Death's in each Note,
And ſure Deſtruction breathes from every throat.
A Plague lies in each Breath, He hates to meet;
And wiſhes oft, his *Ears* were turn'd to *Feet*.
Yet to his Arts he flies, and all doth uſe,
With which ſo oft he could his Foes abuſe.
The *River*, with his wanton Banks that plays,
Runs not more ſecret, nor more winding Ways,
Nor Dancing *Atoms* change more quick their Round,
Nor *Snow*, that hovers loth to touch the Ground.
But all (alaſs!) in vain his Arts he tries,
In vain Acts over all his Treacheries:
And like thoſe, that would from Diſeaſes run,
He flies a while from what he cannot ſhun:
Nor can He hope to ſcape, thô ne'er ſo fleet,
That Death, that's brought him by an Hundred feet.
For the quick-ſcented Dogs thrô all the Ways,
And thoſe ſtrange Shapes, that cautious *Reynard* plays,
With an unerring Courſe purſue their Chaſe.
Follow him, where no Tract is left behind,
And catch the Scent, that dances in the Wind;
Extract it from the Maſs of other Parts,
And find it, thô mix'd with a thouſand Arts.

Noses so quick and pure, methinks, should find
The Secret tract, an *Angel* leaves behind:
And might with little pains in time be brought
To trace the wandring Passage of a *Thought*!
Thus, while they follow with an eager Cry,
And chase their faint and panting Enemy,
O'th' suddain all was hush'd, and every Throat
In a dull silence choak'd his joyfull Note.
No Shout, nor Noise, did rend the parting Air,
Only the raging Huntsmen fret and swear.
All ply their busie Noses, round they coast
To catch that Scent, which in the Crowd was lost:
Till the Grave * *Talbot* with a *Spanish* pace
The long-lost and neglected Scent doth trace;
Finds what their eager Hast had left behind,
And catch'd it Just dissolving in the Wind.
He gives the *Signal*; strait they follow, all
With their Loud throats do one another call,
And, striving to regain the Time, they'd lost,
With doubled Hast after their *Foe* they post:
And with such winged Speed they now pursue,
The unknown *Foe* is quickly brought to view.
When lo! a mixed Crowd from th' neighbouring Town,
Warn'd by the Noise, tumultuously came down;
All, arm'd with Pitchfork, Spit, Flail, Spade and Pole,
To kill the *Fox*, that had their Poultry stole,
Outnoise the Dogs, and with loud Curses fill
The Air with sound of *Follow, follow, kill*!
" Kill him, cries *One*, he stole my Peckled Hen,
" And got my fatted *Capons* out o'th' Pen.
Another Woman lets her Tongue fly loose,
And cries, " the Thief did kill her Brooding *Goose*.
" My *Cock*, saith One, my *Turkey*, saith *Another*,
" My pretty, Copled, *Pullet*, cries *the tother*,

* One of the Finders.

Then

Then all poor *Reynard* with fell Curses rate ;
With Noises rude and inarticulate.
The Amazed *Fox*, astonish'd at the Noise
Much of the Dogs, more of the Women's Cries ;
Seeing his useless *Arts* no help could show,
Resolves at last to see, what *Force* would doe:
Summons his Vigor, doth new Courage rear,
And down the Wind his even Course doth steer.
So some smooth *River*, loth to leave the Plains,
And those fresh Fields, where Mirth and Pleasure reigns,
In many wandring Turns his Passage takes,
A thousand Stops, a thousand Windings makes:
Plays with his flowry Banks, oft turns his Head
And with full Eyes o'relooks his watry Bed,
Courts every wanton Shade, and feigns Delay,
Untill at last, unable more to stay,
Forc'd by the raging Streams, that do descend,
His direct Course He to the Sea doth bend.
The *Fox* begins ; the Chase they all pursue,
Swift, as wing'd *Thoughts* e're to far Countries flew :
Light's slow to them, the sluggish *Wind* doth stay ;
They catch that Scent, his Wings had bore away.
All that by Force or Courage could be shown,
That could by Swiftness, or by Art be done ;
Th' Industrious *Fox* did for his Safety try ; ----
" But there's no struggling with our Destiny.
He's grown Infectious to himself ; --- They find
His Course by th' fatal Breath, he left behind.
His Breathing brings his Ruine on ; that Breath,
That gives to others Life, to him gives Death.
Death doth from Breathing, or Refraining grow ;
To Breathe is Death, and not to Breathe, is so.
At last the *Fox* unable more to strive,
Unable more their Fury to survive :

Seeing i'th' Dog's approach his certain Fate,
Resolves to sell his Life at a dear rate.
So some great *Hero,* compass'd by his Foes,
Death and Destruction all around him strows:
With fiery Rage on all Opposers flies,
And makes a Bulwark of slain Enemies:
Sure not to Live, unwilling yet to dy,
Till he hath left a dear-bought Victory.
Thus the brave *Fox,* when all his hopes were dead,
And no-way left to hide his loathed Head,
Resolves, he will not unrevenged dy,
Nor fall a tame and heartless Enemy:
With Rage salutes the First; his bloody Jaws
Fix'd on the next, do make the Others pawse,
And keep an awfull Distance; Till they all
With one accord upon their *Foe* do fall.
In vain he strives, in vain he fights; for soon
Being by the Raging Tempest overthrown:
He with a faint and trembling Voice doth cry;
"I liv'd by *Rapine* and by *Rapine* dy.

On a Mandrake.

I.

THE Play of *Nature* under ground,
The Draught, that from her Hands doth fall
In Regions, where no Light is found,
But Sullen Darkness Covers all:
Like *Man*; as like, as *Draughts* could be;
Where *Nature* had no Eyes to see.

II.

Each Limb and Part exactly drawn,
Doth much our Admiration raise;
Nature her Mimick Art hath shown,
And wantonly with Mankind plays:

And,

And, thô it may seem useless, yet
The very *Sex* She don't omit.

III.

In this the Picture doth excell,
And doth above the Substance rise:
The *Mandrake* doth in Regions dwell,
Unseen, unknown to Mortal Eyes;
And, where our final Rest we have;
Doth Live and Flourish, in the *Grave*.

On Man's *unhappy Composition.*

UNhappy Man! how ill in Thee are Join'd,
A *Feeble* Body, and an *Active* Mind.
A *Soul* of Fire, a *Body* but of Earth;
That do from different Regions draw their Birth:
One Natu'rally doth tend to Heaven above;
Th' Other tow'rd Earth, from whence it came, doth move.
When such Discordant Parts in Man do meet,
They Justle and each other roughly Greet:
The Motions of the *Soul* the *Body* sway;
Which every Nod and Impulse should obey:
But at each Sally of the Towring *Mind*,
With wearied Journeys *That* doth lag behind.

Thoughts are our Plagues; the Beasts, that none do know,
Are Free from trouble and resentment too.
As *Nature* bids, they every thing receive,
And take it, as her Bounteous Hand doth give.
No pining Thoughts do sowre the Joys, they tast;
No preying Passion doth *their* Body wast;
While *Ours* by the Souls Motion's worn so thin;
'Twill scarce keep Life, and Breath, Life's Tenant, in.
At Things above *Ambition* makes us Soar,
And grasp at what is plac'd beyond our Power: Our

Our feeble Strength we ne'r consult: And then
No wonder, We are tumbled back again.
A chain of Sorrows hangs upon our State:
We for Impossibilities do wait,
Anxiously seek for what will never come,
And yet are angry, when We meet our Doom.
The fault doth not in outward Causes ly,
But in our Judgment, that is warp'd awry.
Our Power's confin'd, and we should Happy be,
If We the Limits of our Power could see.
If We could fix our wandring Thoughts at home,
Nor let beyond our Sphear our Wishes roam,
All things, We see, are Passive here below,
Nor from themselves their Power-to-act doth flow,
They'r dead, unless some greater Essence give
Influx of being, that may make them Live.
'Tis only Heaven doth purely act, and can,
Crumble in Dust the vast Designs of *Man*:
His Will must stand, whatever *We* Design,
Nothing can stop the course of things Divine.
All Aids are useless; what is *Infinite*,
Doth need no Help, nor doth Increase admit.

How Happy *Man*, was He intirely One,
Nor did admit of Composition;
Was his *Æthereal* Soul of Heavenly breed,
Like *Angels*, from the clogs of *Matter* freed:
Or, like the *Beasts*, only with Flesh array'd,
And only of unthinking *Matter* made.
One State would all his Hopes and Thoughts exceed;
By *th' Other* He would from all Care be freed.
Excess of Joy in One his Soul would Crown;
In th' Other *Ignorance* all Fears would drown.

The Sceptick, *against* Mechanism.

LEarning lies deep, and short is Reason's Line,
And weakly do we guess at things Divine!
When those near hand our strict Discovery fly,
What Hopes to dive into *Infinity?*
The Soul's a Particle of Heavenly fire,
And boldly doth to every thing aspire:
But yet how low Her lofty Flights do fall;
When She attempts the Wonders of this Ball!
Our Apprehension *Angels* do exceed,
Like Thought, they can to distant Regions speed,
Nor helps They for Progressive Motion need.
Yet Mysteries, deep hid, they cannot find,
Such as Exceed th' *Intelligences* Mind,
And render all created Beings Blind.
No more, vain Friend, your useless Knowledge show,
Lost in *Abysses*, that no bottom know:
Lapp'd up in Shades, where not one cheerfull Ray
Amid the dismal Darkness points out day.
I grant your Skill,---but how far doth it reach;
Or what import the Mysteries, you teach?
If solid Orbs cramp up the Heaven above,
Or if they Free i'th' fluid *Æther* move:
What unseen Spring to them doth Motion give?
Leave these to those, who in those Regions Live,
How the *Sun's* piercing fire and genial heat,
Doth *Mettals* under Massy Rocks beget;
What are the *Marchasites*, of which they'r made,
And changing *Salts*, in the Composure laid:
How *Heat* Course Mettals into *Gold* refines,
(The Art for which the broyling *Chymist* pines)
Leave this (if such there be) to *Dæmons* of the Mines.

How

How *Orient* Pearls from Heavenly Dew are bred,
And, by what They at first were made, are fed.
The Wonders that in *Neptune's* Storehouse be,
The ragged *Sea-calves* better know, than *We.*
Thou think'st to search all with thy narrow Mind;
The Grasp's too wide for what is so confin'd.
Be Man: And if thou can'st, Inform me how
This Tree, this Flower, this Spire of Grass doth grow:
Why the same Moisture different Shapes doth wear;
Why this doth Green, why this doth Red appear;
Why this doth Fruit, this Flowers, this Herbage bear:
How each a seminal Vertue doth retain,
And, thô not conscious, gets his *Like* again:
Whose *Plastick* Vertue can new Being give,
From whom new Birth, when Dead, they can receive,
And even burnt Flowers can from their Ashes live.
How doth the Imp, when with the Stock 'tis knit,
The Stock's rough Juice to its own Nature fit,
And in the twisted Knot doth sweeten it?
Or Buds of generous Fruits in Wild ones set
A precious off-spring from base Plants beget?
Our Knowledge by the Sence's help we find,
'Tis those deceitfull Guides inform our Mind.
If then the *Medium's* falsе, thrô which Arts go,
How can we hope the genuine Truth to know?
The Water pure and clear i'th' Fountain flows;
But with ill Mixtures doth its Nature lose;
And tasts of every Soil, thrô which it goes.
We from our *Sences* upon trust Receive,
And Them, althô they oft delude, believe.
But Truth and Skill must Disputable grow;
If no account we of our Sences know.
If hidden Secrets in their Nature lie,
That all our diligent Enquiries flie,

If we their Nature strive to search in vain,
What then's the Learning, that by them we gain?
That we do *Hear* and *See*, we all do grant,
But of the manner how, are Ignorant.
If then in things *within* us we may err,
With which each Moment we'er familiar:
What hope remains, that we the Truth should find
Of things *without*, by our deluded Mind?
The Sense deceivs us, and like Painted Glass
Tinges all Objects, that do thrô it pass.
All Sense is made by Contact, You allow:
Contact from unseen Particles doth grow,
Which from all Objects to the Senses flow.
If they'r Material, whence do they arise?
What is't their *Energy* and Force supplies?
Whether they always in the Air do rove,
And wait Impulses, by whose Laws they move?
Or, when they'r wanted, by the *Object* made,
And thence with Message to the *Sense* convey'd?
If these their Subtlety to Motion owe,
Fragments, that from attrited Matter grow,
How happ's it, Time hath not worn all things so?
And why may not succeeding Ages fear,
That Length of Time the Universe should wear,
Till nothing *Solid* in the World appear?
The *Senses* various Particles employ;
What strikes the *Ear*, doth not affect the *Eye*;
And where the *Ear* is deaf, and *Eye* is blind,
The subtle *Smell* can a Sensation find.
The Atoms different, as the Organs are,
And various Forms, various Contextures wear
Besides the different Motions they dispence
From diverse Objects unto every Sense:

By which they to the Judging Soul do show,
Whether they Acceptable are or no.
The *Eye* doth Knowledge of each Colour take,
That various Motions doth i'th' Organ make;
In such Variety, such Cost and Dress,
Not all the Flowers of Rhetorick can express.
But whether What do these Impulses give
Their Power from Angulous Particles receive;
Or barely they This unto Motion owe;
A Secret lies we vainly wish to know.
Since then *Effluviums* from all Objects break,
And thrô the Air their unseen Journeys take,
To every Sense in various Measures come;
How is it that the crowding Troops find room?
Numberless Numbers to each Sense repair,
That various Motions, Forms, and Garbs do wear;
Enough to stifle up the liquid Air.
The justling Streams, always in Motions be,
To all around without Distinction fly.
And from all parts of Matter since they flow,
And heady Journeys in cross Paths do go:
Who in their Passage doth prescribe them Laws?
Or guards them, that they no Confusion cause?
Why do not Storms disperse the Rays of Light,
Why not obstruct their Journey to our sight?
Or those bright Rays, that in clear Days arise,
And from ten thousand Objects cheer our Eyes,
Hinder the Motion of progressive Noise?
In the same Moment from all parts they flow,
Contrary Courses in their Journeys go;
At the same time all Senses gratifie,
Yet we no Battle, nor Confusion spy.
'Tis true they'r Subtle; But they Numerous are:
They'r liquid: Yet the thwarting troops may jarr;
For waves meet waves, & streams with streams do war.

A Guardian *Angel* must be their Defence,
Or we must grant, that Atoms have a Sense.
No humane Force their Fury can restrain;
No giddy Chance their Motion can maintain;
No *Mechanism* their Nature can unfold;
No Laws, nor Rules in Sage's Books enrold.
Nature the *Eye* in beauteous Orbs hath dress'd,
Laid out more Work on't, than on all the rest;
'Tis her much valued Gem, that doth excell
The Treasure, Mines, or Sands, or Seas reveal:
Whose wise Contexture may deep Wits employ,
And hath made Atheists own a Deity.
Man is a *Microcosm*; suppose him One,
The *Eye* is of that *Little-World* the *Sun*.
Heaven's first-born *Light* without this had been lost;
In vain had Nature then been at that Cost,
Yet how this Organ entertains the Light,
And how that wondrous Act is made, the *Sight*.
Whether it Rays receives, or Rays sends-out,
Remains yet an inextricable Doubt.
If th' *Eye* by sending-forth of Rays doth see,
So great Expence what is it can supply?
How do the Srreams make Journeys to the Sky?
For if our Sight we on Emission ground,
We must lend Rays to fill the World around;
These too to' each Object must adapted be
And Images bring back, by which we see.
In vain, what Life and Light doth give, the *Sun*
His annual and dayly Course doth run;
In vain his chearfull Beams doth send: If we
Can from our Selves the want of Rays supply.
If we do from our Selves send Beams of Light;
What is the Difference betwixt Day and Night?
This then's untenable ----- -----

Yet if the Organ by Reception see,
How flows the Poison from an Envious Eye?
How do his *Opticks* venemous Beams instill,
And Great Men in the height of Glory kill?
Whence hath the *Basilisk* his deadly Ray;
That can th' unwary Wretch at distance slay?
How is't, if Wolves first upon Men do look,
Men are with Hoarsness, or with Dumbness strook?
Whence are the Charms flow from a Beauteous Eye?
That do the strugling Slave in Fetters tie?
What *Energy* doth thrô his Vitals move;
What Magick Charm doth stirr him up to Love?
When Thoughts on winged Particles advance,
When piercing Looks the Lover's mutually entrance,
And their Souls on the fiery Atoms dance?
How is it *Cats* and *Owls* see in the Night,
When no Ray can illuminate the Sight.
Their Eyes in Darkness shine; why may not We
Inferr, that they by their own Beams do see?
  This Object is a Central Point, from whence
Rays move around the whole Circumference:
To all about, where e're they'r plac'd, do flie;
In every station, do salute the Eye.
Th' adjoining Atom is a Center too,
From whence in equal streams the Rays do flow.
Ten thousand Objects entertain the Eye;
From each ten thousand thousand Beams do fly.
Since in straight Lines the Rays of Sight are led,
How are they truly to the Eye convey'd?
Why don't the Numbers in each way that rove,
The direct Course of steady Beams remove?
Why is no End unto their Motion put;
When they each other Infinitely cut?
  But yet admit, they to the Eye arrive,
Who of their Nature can a Reason give!

Do they each Moment from the *Sun* repair;
Or have they ſetled Manſions in the Air?
If One; they ſwifter far than Matter move,
Their Nature from their extract they improve,
And ſeem a *Quinteſſence* ſent from above.
What Nouriſhment muſt the vaſt Fount ſupply;
From whence ſuch Streams inceſſantly do fly,
And fill the Liquid Air and Spacious Sky?
If from the *Sun* the Beams of Light do flow,
How doth a *Candle* the ſame Office do?
How doth the *Glow-worm* with the *Sun* conteſt,
And Brandiſh forth her Beams, when He's at reſt?
Why's Rotten Wood and Fiſhes Scales ſo Bright?
Why doth Sea-water Sparkle in the Night?
Theſe Subtle Parts, if in the Air they lie,
How haps, i'th' dark that they eſcape our Eye?
And then in Shades of Night why don't We ſee?
If Colour's in the *Superficies* made,
And variouſly, as that reflects, is bred:
If what *abſorps* the Light is *Black*; that *White*,
Which forcibly *Reflects* the Rays of Light;
And all the dreſſes, that the World can ſhow,
Are the compounded Mixtures of theſe two:
Why ſhould two Marble Stones of equal weight,
Poliſh'd alike, equally Smooth and Bright,
Two different Colours wear of *Black* and *White*?
The ſame Contexture, Form, and Parts they ſhow:
From whence in them do different Colours grow?
Admit all Colours, to the Organ brought,
Are by Reflection of the Object wrought:
And Draughts and Schemes preſent Deform'd or Fair,
As they Impulſes rude or pleaſing bear:
From various Parts that various Colours grow,
And all do on the Superficies flow;
For under that the Sight doth nothing know:

Whe-

Whether these Parts, so subtle and refin'd,
That carry the Ideas to the Mind,
Barely by contact do their Acts maintain;
Or do materially invade the Brain,
A pressing doubt doth yet unsolv'd remain.
If these Impulses to the Eye do give,
That thence doth an Account of things receive;
The Sense, that only did from Motion grow,
When Motion sinks and dies, must perish too.
How haps it then, Ideas stay behind,
And, when We please, can paint anew the Mind,
When what created them is fled, like Wind?
If th' Eye into't nothing Material drew,
How is't the Mind can former Objects view,
And dress i'th' Brain the wandring Schemes anew?
How haps, what did unto our Sight advance,
In Dreams again i'th' cheated Soul do dance,
And with fresh Charms the credulous Mind entrance?
Dreams that arise, as all the Learned own,
From confus'd Parts of Bodies seen or known.
If thro the Eye the Vigorous Object darts
Into the Brain these small Aerial Parts;
How are they entertain'd, when Crowds do come?
How do the little narrow Cells make room?
Do all, that to an Object do belong,
Into one Place unmixt with others throng?
If not: how are things past call'd back with ease?
How is, what's gone, remember'd, when We please,
Even *Adjuncts* and *Particularities?*
But if new Streams the former do expell,
How is't of fo mer Days we acts can tell?
The various Turns of Years long-since repeat;
What We've seen acted, what We've read, relate.
If Old and New i'th Brain together crowd,
How is it Room and Peace is them allow'd?

How

How do they and their Equipages come ?
For if Material, they must take up room.
And tract of Time would hoard up such a Crop,
The crowded Atoms would the Channels stop,
And choke the Passages of Vision up.
The *Ear* in winding Labyrinths is laid,
Fit to receive and keep the Sound, is made:
But yet what Mind's so sharp, so deep, so strong.
To tell the Mysteries to this Sense belong ?
What Garbs the fluid Atoms do array
When they our Thoughts to others do convey ?
Whether the Atoms are of different size,
Or but from various Impulses rise ?
When Soft and Melting Streams do flow from Love,
Or Stormy Accents do from Anger move ?
Whence flow the Charms that do to Speech belong,
When *Graces* dance on a beloved Tongue !
Why the same Words from one should Love create,
And from another but ingender Hate ?
Who can the Charms of *Rhetorick* express,
The Tunefull Motions and the Godlike Dress ?
What Magick force the Captiv'd Ear doth ty,
When well plac'd Words from Artfull Lips do fly,
And calm or raise the Mind, as Storms the Sea ?
How these Impulses, that to th' Ear do pass,
Such transports in the heightned Spirits cause ?
The Ferment scarce will cool and sink again,
And Pleasure's more tumultuous, than Pain.
What Motions Speech must to the Ear convey,
Or in how many Forms the Atoms stray ?
Since We can scarcely find two words alike,
But all must diversly the Organ strike.
Some no distinct Idea do create ;
And Some are what We call *Articulate*,

The

The *Birds* have one, the *Beasts* another Tone,
And every Species hath a different one.
Beside from senseless things the various Noise,
That from Collision of their Parts doth rise:
What doth from Solids, what from Fluids flow,
What do from Winds, from Seas, and Thunder grow.
Whence are the Charms, that *Musick* doth dispence;
That lulls in pleasing Slumbers up the Sense?
When Raptures from the Numbers are compil'd,
Which render'd *Alexander* Fierce, or Mild:
Can quell the Lustfull or Revengefull Flame,
Can Bloody Rage and Savage Fury tame:
Can Conquer when all Arguments do fail,
When Reason's Ineffectual, can prevail:
Can Witchcraft's force and Poyson's fire asswage,
And, when all Medicines fail, Disease's Rage.
What Sorcery doth in these Numbers ly,
And what Enchantment from the Sounds doth fly?
The wondrous Art what Learning can explain,
That from mov'd Air doth all its Vertue gain,
And yet so Forcible and Strong, to call
The Senseless Stones to build *Thebe's* stately wall?
Enchanting Art! the Learn'd do own in Thee,
The next great Power unto the Deity.
By Musical Numbers, *Heaven*, they say, was made:
And by their help the *Earth* in Beauty laid.
Reason and Sense do from thy Concords fly,
For th' Human Soul it self's but *Harmony*.
Smelling, Thou subtle Sense, what th' *Eye* can't see,
Nor doth within the Sphear of *Hearing* lie;
What no Brisk Sallyes, no Impulses brings,
But silent lies hid in the Mass of things;
Thy secret Art can thrô all Mazes find,
Thô with confused Heaps of Parts combin'd.----

But how 'tis done, a Myſt'ry yet remains
That Baffles all our curious Wit and Pains.
How is it the Sagacious *Hound* doth find
The unſeen Parts, that mix with Air and Wind?
When with a trembling fear the *Prey* doth fly,
Employs his eager ſpeed to' outſtrip the Eye,
And hopes, that done, no farther Danger's nigh.
How is't, the Wind don't the Compoſure break,
And all the chaïn of Steames in pieces ſhake?
What doth thoſe Parts from mixed Heaps extract,
And render the disjointed Parts exact?
How doth the *Hound* purſue, when no tract's ſhown,
And keep the ſteady Path, where no Guide's known?
Thô others of the Kind the footſteps tread,
The mixture cannot Him to Errour lead:
How are the Kindred Vapours ſevered?
How doth He follow what at firſt He trac'd,
And Hunt without diſtraction to the laſt;
And all the bragging *Chymiſt's* Art ſurpaſs,---
Who, when mix'd Mettals do compound one Maſs,
In time, by Pains, and by the help of Fire,
Each Mettal can extract and render each entire.
How is't, the *Vultur* hath ſo quick a ſmell,
He can in diſtant Realms of Battels tell;
And Slaughters at three hundred Leagues reveal?
How do the Particles of *Smell* come whole,
That muſt ſo far o'r Seas and Mountains rowl?
Who gives them Knowledge to find out the Way?
How haps, they are not wilder'd, while they ſtray,
Or loſt, when they muſt mix with thoſe of *Land*, or *Sea*?
How is it, Peſtilential Vapours fly?
Why fix on this, and why the next paſs by?
How Poyſon they in pleaſing Odours breath,
And while We ſuck Delight, We draw in Death.

No Light of Sense or Reason can descry,
What Steames from *Aromatick* Bodies fly :
When different Bodies different Odours cast,
And these Effluvium's are unlike the last.
How is it Gums such Streams of sweet diffuse ;
And yet in Bulk or Weight do nothing loose ?
Thô many Ages they to last are found,
With Odorous Parts incessantly abound,
Impregnate all the Sphear of Air around.
Yet for so great Fxpence, no great Decrease,
Nor do they grow proportionably less.
Now if these Atoms are Material, why,
Since they the small parts of the Compound be,
Doth not the *Whole* at length by parcels die ?
Do they a secret unknown Vertue bear ;
To change into their Kind the Ambient Air :
As all, Fire meets, doth his fierce Nature wear ?
As *Load-stones* in the *Iron* their Vertue leave ;
For what they touch, to *Iron* again will cleave ?
Or do the Odours, that they thus disclose,
When they have circled round, i'th' Drugs repose ?
In their first Parent loose themselves again,
And so their Odour, Bulk, and Weight maintain ?
As Tapers in fast-closed Urnes are found,---
(Whose Circling Rays do move for ever round)
To feed on Unctuous Fumes, they from them cast ;
Supply themselves, and so can never wast.
I pass the Doubts, that ly i'th' Sense of *Tast* :
And those as great, that are in *Feeling* plac'd.
For wheresoe'r We look's an unknown Coast,
Our Mind perplex'd in endless Storms is tost;
And in th' *Abyss* all Wit and Learning lost.
There may more *Senses* be, that yet We want,
Whose Absence renders Us so Ignorant.

We known't, how high *Angelick* Senſe doth riſe,
Nor what th' Intelligences makes ſo wiſe.
We wondrous Acts done by the Creatures ſee,
Nor can We tell, but they new *Senſes* be.
What makes the *Cock* at his due Seaſons crow,
And Time of Midnight ſo exactly know?
How doth the *Halcyon* future Calmes preſage,
And how Sea fowl approaching Tempeſt's Rage?
When they to *Iſles* retire, and Seamen ſhow
(Their Hate and Terrour) Storms before they blow.
Why Palms do flouriſh, when to Palms they'r nigh;
And when they'r parted, or decay, or die?
How doth the *Needle* his dear *North* purſue,
What *Senſe* doth learn him to be ever true?
Why doth the *Magnet* his Courſe *Iron* enfold,
Nor can be Brib'd by what's more Precious, *Gold*?
The Subjects that for *Sympathy* are fam'd,
And what by Us *Antipathies* are nam'd,
May different *Senſes* be; and ſo may thoſe,
Whoſe Nature all our Learning can't diſcloſe;
That do above our Ignorant darkneſs riſe,
Loſt in the name of *Occult-Qualities*,
Th' *Aſylum* of the *Slothfull* or *Unwiſe*.

Boaſt of thy *Mechaniſm*, vain Friend, no more;
Nor think theſe Depths by Reaſon to explore.
Fix on what Part Thou wilt in all the Round,
Queſtions ariſe, thy Wiſdom will confound.
What may Opinions try, no *Standard's* known,
Where Genuine Truth from falſhood may be ſhown;
But gloomy Miſts over the Mind do rowl,
And Prejudice doth prepoſſeſs the Soul.
All here we know's but *Probability*,
The Utmoſt Bound, to which our Wit can fly,
And that which Terminates *Philoſophy*.

One Starts a *Wit*; the Schools his Schemes allow;
Untill *Another* Specious grounds doth show,
And doth the long-built *Fabrick* overthrow.
All strive for Empire, both in *State* and *Wit*,
He's Victor, unto whom the rest submit.
But here's the Fate of Both, Both slippery stand,
And yield to th' next Intruder their Command.
How wretched 'tis to trust on Chance, that's blind!
It brings no Comfort to the doubtfull Mind.
The Human Soul can't rest on such a Guide,
Nor's with unthinking Matter satisfied.
No Truth from Principles so weak can flow,
The more We search, the Darker still We grow.
Doubts after Doubts arise, and when one's done,
New Crowding Numbers hastning hurry on.
And what appēar'd a Trifle to our Mind,
At nearer insight We a Mystery find.
So Countries seem to *Seamen* from the shore
But small; yet when they farther do explore,
They find with stretch'd-out Arms the widened Coast;
Till the bold Eye is in the Prospect lost.
A Wise, Just, *Being* over all presides,
The turns of Stupid Thoughtless Matter guides;
Whose boundless *Wisdom* knows to govern all
The Startling Wonders of this changing *Ball*.
In *Him* Man's Happy and his Soul at rest;
Doubts are husht up and Peace becalms the breast.
Courage on his Alliance doth depend;
In Him our anxious Fears and Terrours end.
" We in the *Deity* alone can rest,
" And in that *Acquiescence* must be blest.

A Pin

A Pindarique *Ode in Praise of* Angling.

To My Worthy Friend Mr. Thomas Bateman.

STANZA I.

W*Ater*, thou mighty Universal Good,
Thou Mother of *Fertility*;
Thou *Nature's* Vital Blood!
That thrô Earth's crooked Veins dost slide,
Thrô secret Caverns and dark Ways dost glide;
And with thy Kindly Influence
Dost Life and Vigour to the Whole dispence:
Thy Power doth thrô all Parts of Nature wind;
All, that we *Feel*, or *Smell*, or *Tast*, or *See*,
All owe their Birth and Growth to *Thee*!
Thy Moisture doth the parts of Bodies join,
Hard *Rocks* and *Adamants* thy Vertue find:
An unseen Balm each Particle doth tie,
Doth them in lasting *Friendship* twine;
Which, when by *Chymick* Art extracted thence,
The separated *Parts* do all
To scorned Dust and Rubbish fall:
Wisely did *Thales* Thee the Sourse of All things call!

II.

Old Fainting *Nature* thou dost keep alive;
With pleasing *Cordial* dost her strength retrieve,
Which she doth thirstily drink down.
And th' Age shall come, as Sacred *Bards* have told,
Which they in Heaven's high Laws have found enrol'd;
When Heat shall th' Earth's *Balsamick* Moisture sink,
Insatiate Heat the *Radical Moisture* drink;

And

And th' Feaverish World shall burn and fry
Deliquiums and strange *Syncopes* endure
Till th' *Hectick* Fire beyond all Medicine grown,
The Circling *Zodiack* shall in pieces fly
And melted by the rageing *Calenture*,
Th' Eternal *Poles* shall sink and all
The Massy Rocks, the Earth's Foundation
Into the deep-wrought Pit of sure Destruction fall.

III.

Bless'd *Element*! How gratefull to my Mind!
Nurse of Delight and pleasing Joy!
What Charms can I in thy Embraces find!
No wonder wise Antiquity
Did Beauteous Nymphs to *Chrystal* Rivers turn;
And made their Lovers i'th' cool Streams to burn,
Enchanting Goddess! without Thee
The World would all a *Lybian* Desert be;
Hot scalding Sands would o're its Surface spread,
And noxious Beasts and pois'nous Serpents breed.
Thou deck'st the Lovers shady Bowers,
Thou dressest up the Meads with Flowers;
Thy four-fold Streams thrô Paradise did run
Dress'd by the Hand Divine,
Silver'd by Thee, and *Gilded* by the Sun.
Ceres to Thee her Growth doth ow;
And *Bacchus* thanks Thee for his Generous Wine,
Bred by the *Sun* and thy sweet Flowers!
And Gods to Thee their Gratitude should show,
From whom their *Nectar* and *Ambrosia* flow!

IV.

Here in *Elysian* Fields by chiding Rills
The Off-spring o'th' eternal Hills;
Beneath a pleasing Shade, that can defeat
The *Sun's* impetuous Heat;

Where *Zephyr* gently murmurs thrô the Bowers,
And dallies with the smiling Flowers,
And all the winged *Choristers* above
In melting strains sing to the God of *Love*:
While pleased *Nature* doth a silence keep,
Even Hills do Nod, and Rivers seem to Sleep:
Here with a *Friend*, Copartner of my Joys,
Whose Artfull Soul knows every way
The scaly Off-spring to betray,
The bold, the fearfull, or the cautious *Prey*:
I an extensive Empire lay
O're all the watry Plain;
And numerous Subjects do our Scepters fear.
SALMON, the King of Rivers, that each Year
Removes his watry Court to th' Sea;
But with the *Sun* and Spring returns again,
And o're all Bars of Art, or Nature, flies,
O're Floodgates, Wears and Rocks his Course doth steer.
And if the *Alpes* in's Passage lay
Like *Hannibal* would find, or force, a Way.
The Beauteous *TROUT*, of the same Princely Blood,
But of a less Estate and kept at Home,
Confin'd to his own narrow Flood,
Can't with such State o're distant Regions roam.
In his own fenced Court secure he lies;
Till by some treacherous Bait betray'd, he dies.
The ravenous *PYKE*, the River-*Wolf*, whose Throat
Like Hell promiscuously all swallows down;
Bold and Rapacious a great Tyrant reigns
O're all the Subjects of the watry Plains.
No Kind hath an Exemption got;
To him no Rule of Love or Kind.ed's known:
The Fury of his Jaws not his own Race can shun.

V. With

V.

With these the armed *PEARCH*, that dares
Even with the Tyrant *Pyke* make wars,
And doth a petty Empire own
O're all the lesser Fry;
Delicious Food to curious Palates known.
BREAM, that i'th' calmy Deeps doth lie
And at great Banquets makes a Dish of State.
BARBELL, the River-Swine,
That doth i'th' watry Regions root and eat:
In hollow Rocks doth place his Seat,
By Floodgates, Cataracts, and Bridges lies,
And all the Force of sweeping Nets defies.
CHEVIN, that under shady Boughs doth play,
And's kill'd more for Delight and Sport, than Prey;
On whom the Hungry even unwilling dine.

VI.

HUMBER and *GREYLING*, that swift streams do love
Of *Derwent*, Fruitfull *Trent*, and Chrystal *Dove*.
CARP even by Princes priz'd, whom curious Tasts approve;
In fenced Ponds, safe as a Treasure laid,
The Stream's Physician *TENCH*, whose balmy Slime
Heals all the Maladies of the watry Clime.
The silver *EEL*, that yet doth keep unknown
Her Secret way of Propagation:
These and a Crowd of *Species* more
That live on many a distant Shore;
Some that in *Beauty* do exceed;
Some that in *Strength* and some in *Speed*:
And some by Nature arm'd for bloody *Fight*.
Some that in fertil *Mudd* do feed,
Some that in barren *Sands* delight,
Some that fenc'd *Rocks* and woody Shades do own:
Beside the ignoble lesser Fry,

The

The *Rabble* of the watry Clime,
Not worth a Fisher's Time,
And more unworthy Memory,
Destin'd by Fate the Greater's Prey to be.
I'th' Water's curs'd *Democrasie*,
Are Subjects all of our Dominion.

VII.

With artfull Hand and with judicious Eye
We sleave the Artificial *Fly*.
Nature, the Universal Guide,
In every step and progress She doth make,
Our *Art* can overtake:
There's not an Insect, dress'd in all the Pride,
In all the pompous gawdy Pageantry,
That *Nature's* Wardrobe can create,
But our unbounded *Art* can imitate.
All, that on Plants, or Simples breed,
All, that on Trees, or Waters feed;
All, that the fruitfull Spring,
The *Sun* and *Heat* do to Perfection bring;
All, that do grow from Putrefaction:
Each Colour, Shade, and Shape, that's made
I'th' Universal Shop, where lie
The Molds, in which each Creature's laid
And Garbs, each Insect do invest,
Our Artfull Bait puts on,
By a quick Eye and a rich Fancy drest.
So true, it can't Distinguish'd be
By *Trout* or *Greyling's* piercing Eye.

VIII.

With Art contriv'd, manag'd with Art, the *Fly*
By steady Hand and nimble Eye,
To any distant Place we throw;
And th' fatal Bait to credulous Eyes do show:

. VVary, as Treaſon lurks, we move
Silence do all Conſpiracies improve.
The deadly Bait ſhakes pendent in the Air,
Deadly and fatal, as a Blazing ſtar,
Deſtruction with it falls to all, are near:
Infectious Influence it doth breathe
None can its Charms deny:
" So ſteep and ſlippery are the Ways to Death.

IX.

Sometimes in pitty to the watry Race
Our generous Endeavours preſs
To kill the Raving Tyrant of the Flood
The *Pyke*, that his own Subjects makes his Food;
Waylays the Streams and beaten Roads
And common ways to their Aboads,
And all, that in his Reach do come,
Do in his hungry Entrails find a Tomb.
Hunger, that Death to all about doth breathe,
Fatal to him doth his own Death bequeath:
A Captive Fiſh in Chains we tie;
Which, *Decius*-like, with comely State
Doth for his Kindred's ſafety boaſt to die:
With all inviting Motions plays,
That may deſire and hunger raiſe,
And draw the *Tyrant* to the deadly Bait:
And how doth he rejoyce,
To periſh with him in one common Fate?
While all the Kindred Fry,
In crowding Shoals expreſs their Joy,
That now untroubled *Peace* doth o're the Waters fly

X.

Of Old —— —— —— ——
The happy Man, that did a Tyrant ſlay,
And a ſlav'd People to their Freedom bring;
Or He, that from ſome deadly Dragon's Sting,

Or bloody Jaws of Beasts of Prey
The frighted Multitude did free;
Each joyfull Mouth did sing his Praise,
With honour'd Wreaths each hand his Head did crown:
Statues and Obelisks the Crowd did raise;
And Garlands on Triumphant Arches nod;
And the next Age made him a God:
Thus *Python's* Death *Apollo's* Godhead gave;
And *Hydra* slain render'd *Alcides* Brave.
What Honour then to Us belongs,
What Praises, and what just Renown,
Who th' watry Race from their Great *Tyrant* save?
The watry Race, whose silent Tongues
Cannot in melting Numbers Pray,
Nor Thanks for Favours lent repay!
Mean Souls may long Intreaties love,
Them Prospects of Rewards may move:
That Favor's Great, which without these is Generously done.

XI.

Sometimes with patient Skill
We watch the Motion of our trembling Quill:
No Force, nor Tyranny we use;
Each Fish, or may accept, or may refuse:
And no One's took, but he that will.
All the inviting Baits we prove,
Which Nature naked doth present,
Or Art, her Handmaid, doth improve:
And if we find their Stomacks low
All Dainties, that on Nature's Bosom grow,
And all sweet melting Pasts we use;
Rich, *Aromatick*, Drugs infuse
With cleanly Art and Neatness spent:
(Cleanliness much the watry Race doth love,
Who every moment wash their Filth away.)

All, that may pleaſe their curious Scent,
Or their more-curious Eye ;
That thoſe, whom *Hunger* doth not move,
Are took by *Wantonneſs* and *Curioſity*:

XII.

Bleſs'd Art ! for Contemplation fit,
And towring Sallys of the Mind ;
Where *Fancy* free and unconfin'd,
To diſtant Objects takes her Flight.
Sometimes from ſtreams in humble Vales below
We to th' Celeſtial *Cataracts* do riſe,
And viſit all the Scaly Race
That ſtreams, above-the-Firmament, do grace,
And Angle with a *Jacob's* Staff !
Now we to meaner Subjects bow,
On our own *Chryſtal* Rivers gaze,
And ſee the World decipher'd in the Glaſs,
And at its ſerious Follies laugh !
See *Tyranny* i'th' Ravenous *Pyke* is ſhown,
I'th' Armed *Pearch Oppreſſion*,
And in the Servile Crowd *Paſſive* Subjection;
The Servile Crowd, that ne'r of Wrongs complain,
Curs'd *Democratick* State ; ----
That doth no Law or Precepts own,
But headlong Fury over all doth reign.
And all the leſſer Fry
Without or Crime, or Cauſe, muſt dy,
Onely becauſe they'r Small and others Great.

XIII.

Raptur'd Delight ! the Soul, that loves not Thee
Whom Fatal Pleaſures o'th' Deceitfull Court,
Or *Sycophantick* Flattery,
Whom Riches, or whom Honours ſway,
Or whom Revenge doth draw away,

Or other low or base Design mislead
From thy serener Sport;
May He upon some naked Beach,
That o'r those Streams doth hang, he cannot reach,
Or may he in a *Lybian* Desert dwell
With burning rowling Sands o'respread,
One Degree on this side Hell:
May he among the Cinders live and burn,
Till he a perfect *Salamander* turn:
With raging Thirst for cooling Currents long,
But never get one Drop to cool his Tongue.
And if a Fish he e'r doth chance to see,
May it a *Crocodile* or *Hydra* be:
May scaly Serpents round his Temples twine,
Serpents, whose Heat
Their blood doth up to Poyson boil:
May *Asps* and *Adders* be his Meat,
And blood of *Dragons* be his Wine;
May He far off behold a flowry Plain,
And winding Rivers thrô it smile,
Like *Tantalus* to' increase his pain;
May these to him be seen,
As to the Damn'd the Joys of Heaven, with a vast Gulf be-(tween!
May all these Plagues doubled to him resort,
That any Poaching Ways doth use,
Or th' Honour of our Art abuse,
Or with devouring Nets doth spoil our Sport.

XIV.

May I (far from desire of being Great)
Enjoy a little Quiet Seat,
That overlooks a *Chrystal* Stream:
With Mind as Calm, as is her Brow,
Pure as the Fountain, whence her Waters flow;
Those Pleasures tast a *Cynick* could not blame.

And

And may (Ye watry *Sisters* all,
With Fruitfulness and Plenty crown'd)
May all your Dewy Blessings on Me fall!
Ye, that from craggy Rocks do take Your Source,
Or from the Flowry Hills do grow:
All, that in hollow Vaults resound,
Or do from Fruitfull Valleys flow:
All, that thrô Rocks Your way do force,
And foaming Waves in pieces dash;
All, that in Flowry Meadows stray,
And with Your Amorous Banks do play;
All, whose proud Waves the Walls of Citties wash;
All, that thrô Deserts take Your Course.
All, whose wide Bosoms *Ships* do plow,
Which *Vice* and *Riches* bring:
All, that to humble Cotes do bow,
And hear the Jolly Shepherds, when they sing:
The Haughty, Rapid, and Imperious Dames;
The Still, the Quiet, and Soft-gliding Streams:
May all assist the *Angler's* harmless Sport,
And with Full Hands unto Our Line Resort;
All, that with Silver Feet
In Melting Numbers and Harmonious Strains,
Immortal *Spencer* once did cause to meet
On th' Marriage-Day of *Medway* and of *Thames*!

On the Honourable the Countess Dowager OF GAINSBOROW, *&c.*

EMbodied Vertue, Light of Humane Race,
Your Age's Glory and Your Sexe's Grace,
Whose Fair Example *Vice* it self might move
To be a *Proselyte* to Vertuous Love.
And ah! what Sinner could the Force oppose;
When *Vertue* from so strict a *Beauty* flows,
Beauty, that double Charms on Worth bestows.
Lately the World of Your Rare Wedlock rang,
And Angels of the Nuptial Concord sang,
When a *Male Vertue* equally was plac'd
With Yours, embracing and alike Embrac'd;
Two Souls in one Dissolving Rapture couch'd,
With the same *Magnet* Two blest Souls were touch'd;
So Just the Flame, so Equal the Desire;
As if One Soul two Bodies did inspire
Not with a *Raging*, but a *Lambent*, Fire.
This Mutual Friendship all admiring saw,
And Glorious Copies thence began to draw;
When ah! the Generous *Heroe* sank away,
Remorceless Death seiz'd the Illustrious Prey,
And left Your Single Light to gild our Day.
Thus when the shining *Monarch* of the Skies,
Below the *Western* Mountains faints and Dies;
Singly the silver *Moon* his Place supplies.

Ten.

Ten thousand Luminaries round Her wait,
And silently adore Her Princely State:
Above them all the Beauteous Goddess goes,
And Gracious Beams on her Attendants throws:
The Gladsome World approve Her Empire well,----
And now scarce miss the *Sun*, That but so lately fell.

THE SUBMARINE VOYAGE.

A Pindarick Poem IN FOUR PARTS.

By Tho. Heyrick, M. A. *Formerly of* Peter-*House College in* Cambridge.

Πωλεῖταί τις δεῦρο [Νέων] ἅλιος Νημερτὴς
Ἀθάνατος, Πρωτεὺς, ——— Ὅς τε θαλάσσης
Πάσης βένθεα οἶδε, Ποσειδάωνος Ὑποδμώς.

Homer. Odyss. Δ. V. 384. &c.

CAMBRIDGE,
Printed by *John Hayes*, for the Author,
M. DC. XCI.

To the Right Honourable

JOHN Lord *ROOS* *Eldest-Son* To the Earl of *RUTLAND, &c.*

My Lord,

THIS Poem, *drawn by the loud Fame of Your* Learning *and* Candour, *comes from the remotest Parts of the World to fall down at your Honour's Feet; there being not one Part of the* Earth *or* Sea, *which is not fill'd with the Report of Your Goodness, and which doth not know, that Your Family is the* Asylum *of* Arts *and* Arms. *It hath pass'd safely the* Northern *Snows, and* Southern *Fires; nor hath it been swallow'd up in the merciless Gulf. It hath been preserv'd from the Savage Monsters of the Sea, and the as-savage* Indian *Cannibals. It hath visited both* Indies, *and it would be too hard a Fate to have it suffer Shipwrack in the Port. It flies to You for Protection from a sort of Monsters,*

Africk *never bred, nor the* Indies *are acquainted with; whom the Sea never produc'd, nor can shew in its Depths and Abysses,* viz. *those* Momes, *whose strength lies not in their Teeth, but their Tongue; who kill not for Hunger, but Malice; and whose Words are like the pois'ned Arrows of the* Indians. *It hath seen the greatest Rarities in the World, which it finds outdone in Your Self; and with an admiration, it never was touch'd with before, begs leave to adore those Perfections, which it is not in the power of Words to express. Which if Your Honour vouchsafe, it will be the greatest Credit and Security, that a Mortal Muse could ever deserve, or desire; and consequently an Eternal and Weighty Obligation to*

(My Lord)

Your Honour's

Most Humble and

Obliged Servant

THO. HEYRICK.

The Submarine Voyage.

A PINDARIQUE Ode.

PART I.

STANZA I.

UPON a Promontory's Point,
That ſtretch'd out far into the Sea;
That of perpetual War had bore the dint,
Of foming Waves, and angry Surges ſway:
A Deſolate and lonely Place,
Where *Seales* ſecurely play'd,
And feathered Fowl their winged off-ſpring laid;
But unfrequented by all Human Race,
I ſtood: By wild Meanders thither led,
My wearied Feet had wandred with my Head,
Loſt in the Maze of thought:
Steep headlong Cliffs my eager footſteps ſtayd,
And I a Scene of Seas ſurvey'd,
Which mixed Fear and Pleaſure brought:
Whoſe beauteous Boſom ſmooth and fair,
Did all the charms and flattery wear,
With which ſhe us'd to cheat the credulous Mariner;
When Smiling ſhe invited to betray.
The Wanton waves did with the Sun-beams play:
(If any Waves did there appear)

The

The liquid Plains were folded up to reſt.
The wars of Nature ſeem'd to ſleep:
Peace ſtretch'd her Downy feathers o're the Deep,
And the calm-brooding *Halcyon* built her Neſt.

II.

A Sail far off dreſs'd in the height of pride
Top and Top-Gallant did in triumph ride:
The ſubject Waves did groan beneath the weight,
Which ſoon ſhould by the Change of Fate,
(Such a Viciſſitude of things is laid)
Exalt themſelves above her Lofty head.
The careleſs Crue within in Mirth and Joy
Their few ſhort Moments did employ,
Nor e're dream'd of their haſt'ning Deſtiny.
For lo! a ſuddain Storm did rend the Air:
The ſullen Heaven, curling in frowns its brow,
Did dire preſaging Omens ſhow;
Ill-boding *Helena* alone was there.
The ſtarting Sun deny'd his Light,
Not willing to behold the ſight;
Nothing ſo mercileſs as Night!
Mountainous Waves came crowding from afar,
That threatned even to Heaven a War.
The bonds of Nature ſeemed broak,
And her foundations with the Tempeſt ſhook:
As thô the looſe diſjoynted World
Was to be once more in a Chaos hurl'd.
The labouring Bark in vain doth ſtrive
In Cataracts of Seas to live;
Her Mizen's gone, the Sail-yard cracks,
Her Rudder's loſt, the Mainmaſt breaks:
On the deaf Gods in vain they call,
The Gods to their own Empire look,
Are more with Fear than Pitty ſtrook,

And the Tenth wave doth fink them all.
Into the vaſt Abyſs they fall — —
They and their Great Deſigns:
The hopes of Merchandiſe and Gain,
The Dear-bought price of Dangerous pain,
Their Golden dreams of undiſcover'd Mines.

III.

Bleſs me! cry'd I, what dubious Fate
On mortall Men doth wait.
Blindly in deadly Paths we walk,
The Meſſengers of Death about us ſtalk;
Unſeen their Ambuſhments are laid,
Arreſt us, when there ſeems leaſt cauſe of Dread.
In other things alike; with anxious Pain
We ſtrive Diſcoveries to gain,
Which mock our wearied Expectation.
Skin-deep we only pierce, and what's behind
Is unknown Regions, we can never find:
The floting Iſlands ſhow themſelves and then they'r gone.

IV.

How deſpicable is our State below;
What fetters choak the ſoaring Mind:
Little of Truth in all the Maſs we find,
That may Rewards on Painfull years beſtow.
Dark Miſts and Errours us ſurround,
We walk upon Enchanted ground,
Spectres and Phantôms fill the Round.
Mormoes dreſs'd up in Antick ſhapes appear,
And what we graſp but fills our Arms with Air.
With wandring Eyes we Heaven behold,
And ſee the ſtarry Orbs from far,
Percieve that they are rowl'd,
But yet the hidden Wheels a Secret are.

From

From what Materials they are bred;
Their Diſtance and their Magnitude;
And if they be inhabited, ———
Are ſecrets that our Minds elude.

V.

So we the ſurface of the Earth behold:
Where Joy and Plenty hath her Boſom crown'd,
Where burning Sands do curſe the Barren ground:
Where with Prolifick heat ſhe ſmiles,
And where ſhe's fetter'd up with cold:
Where Craggy rocks lift their aſpiring head;
Where ſhe ſinks down into a fruitfull Mead,
And with ſoft joy the Mind beguiles:
Where Beauteous Nymphs with ſilver feet do tread:
We ſee her Civil and her Antick dreſs,
Where ſhe's a Paradiſe, and where a Wilderneſs.

VI.

But this our Knowledge and our Sight confines,
What is below's a Secret made:
Where Precious ſtones in hidden beds are laid;
Where Quarries riſe or Rivers wind,
That under Mighty rocks their paſſage find;
Or where's the Seat of undiſcover'd Mines.
Where Princely Cities once did ſhow their head,
Now in their Ruines buried.
Where Sacred Monuments of Kings were plac'd,
The falſe Repoſitories of the dead,
By Eating Time defac'd.
What is betwixt us and the Center ſet,
What are the Rocks, on which the Earth is rais'd:
How they endure the Subterraneous heat,
And keep in bounds the Central fire,
By which at laſt the Fabrick muſt expire.

These

Theſe all are Myſteries, which we can't undoe ;
For when we would below the ſurface know,
Our native Soil an unknown Land doth grow.

VII.

But who of Thee, falſe Element, can ſpeak,
Thou treacherous Sea ! that ſmil'ſt to wrack ?
That doſt new Faces every day put on,
As Variable, as thy Guide, the Moon,
What boundleſs Mind can fathom Thee,
That by thy Changing ſhun'ſt Diſcovery ?
And why, Juſt Heaven, doſt thou long Life beſtow
O'th' ſenceleſs *Hart* and ſtupid *Crow* ;
O'th' *Serpent*, that her Skin can caſt,
And th' *Eagle*, that doth many Ages laſt :
To whom it nothing doth Import ;
That can't to Noble Speculations riſe,
Nor Nature's ſecrets view with ſharp ſagacious Eyes ?
Why ſhould ſwift Change ſnatch man's ſhort Thread away,
That only can due Homage pay,
The great Attendant on thy Court :
And why ſhould *Art* be long, and *Life* be ſhort ?
Why ſhould Amphibious Creatures ſee
What doth to Man a Secret lye ;
Into the Depth of the Abyſs go down,
And in two Empires live, while Man's confin'd to one ?

VIII.

May ſome kind *Genius* gratify
My daring Curioſity,
That would the Seas ſurpriſing Bottom ſee !
The Wonders, Nature ſecret keeps
In her vaſt Storehouſe of the Deeps ;
The various Plants, that Deck the watry Plain ;
The Trees and Shrubs, that it adorn,
And precious Products, that on them are born ;

The massy Heaps of Pearl and Golden Oar,
The working Sea hath driven up in store;
With all the scatter'd Riches of the Main:
The numerous subjects of the Realm of Waves,
The Fountains of the Deep and Subterranean Caves!

IX.

— —— Scarce had I spoke,
When *Neptune* chanc'd my wish to hear,
That's often Deaf to shipwrack'd Wretches Prayer;
And lik'd my bold Ambition well. — —
A sudden Numbness all my Members stroke:
The cheerfull Light, that welcome Comfort gives,
And th' wearied Mind with Joy relieves,
With an unpleasing force my Eyes did strike,
And the Sun's heat I did dislike.
Weary o'th' too-thin piercing Air,
Another Element my thoughts Employs:
The watry Plains I view'd with pleased Eyes.
Fearless the noise of Storms I hear,
The foaming Surges bring no cause of fear;
And Hurricanes become familiar.
I long'd to visit *Neptune*'s Court,
And see the *Tritons* and the Sea-Nymphs sport.
Mean while within a Change I found;
Nature was working some new feat,
And summon'd all her Powers to meet,
Armour of scales enclos'd me round:
My Hands and Legs did nimble Fins display,
That could through yielding Water cut their way.
And from the Cliff, whose Downfall stemm'd the Eye,
And made even starting Nature fly,
Fearless I cast my self into the Sea. —

A Dol-

A *Dolphin* now I sport and play i'th' Main,
Do unto Man my Ancient Love retain:
And Reason still and Curiosity remain.

X.

But oh! what Language doth suffice to tell
The Rapine and Oppression,
The Armed Force and Violence,
That in those liquid Regions dwell?
Justice and Equity were flown,
And Right and Property not known:
No Laws to be the Poor's defence,
No Tenderness to Innocence:
The Less became the Greaters Prey,
Only because they could not fight:
And while these others swallow, They,
And what they had devour'd, became anothers Right
No one by Might or Subtlety's secur'd;
The Greater still commands the Lesser's fate;
Now this devours, and now he is devour'd:
All on unruly Appetite doth wait.
So cursed is an Anarchy
So insupportable Democrasie.
Insatiate Element! how well with Thee
Do thy Inhabitants agree!
Pitty from both of you is banished,
Justice from both of you is fled:
And when you do devour,
You both are hungry still and gape for more.

XI.

There was a Rock that overlook'd the flood,
That the Seas Terminating Pillar stood;

By battering Waves in numerous Ages rent,
Or Earthquake's fury, from the Continent:
Whose Craggy Cliffs no other Race did bear,
But Birds, the wild Inhabitants o'th' Air,
That to the subject Sea for food repair:
Under whose side --whether by Nature's skill
By giddy Chance, or some Diviner will,
Or teeth of Time, or restless Waves, that tear
The hardest Rocks, and steeliest Mountains wear;
And (did not heavenly Powers their fury stay)
Even Nature's fixed Barrs would eat away,
A Cave was form'd --a Refuge for th' oppress'd,
Where injur'd Innocence secure might rest.
'Tis said, when Giants with the Gods did fight,
This shelter'd frighted *Neptune* in his flight:
Since which no armed Force may it invade,
But 'tis for Wretches an *Asylum* made.

XII.

Hither I fled, affrighted at the Sight
Of bleeding Justice and of injur'd Right,
Oppress'd by all-commanding unrelenting Might.
Hither the Love-sick *Tritons* oft did come
And to the Pittiless Rocks lament their doom:
With Mournfull strains their Sea-Nymphs pride rehearse }
To the regardless Rocks in polish'd verse; }
Whose tunefull Accents the rude Waves disperse. }
Here wanton Meremaids often would resort,
And spend the Halcyon days in various sport:
Invent new Arts to make them look more Fair,
Comb and adorn their Green dis-shevell'd Hair.
And here be-nighted *Neptune* sometimes keeps his Court.

XIII. Hence

XIII.

Hence from my Safe Retreat,
With Eyes, that trembled yet for Dread,
I saw the Pearls ly in their Mother-Bed;
From Heavenly Dew and Drops of Night,
And from transparent Moisture bred:
Enlivened by *Sol's* Genial Heat:
How Drop by Drop the Films are made,
Th' Attracted Moisture o'r them spread,
Till they by New Accessions grown,
Adorn'd with Dazling Sparkling Light,
Are fit to' Inrich an Haughty Monarch's Crown.
The useless, undisturbed Store,
No Savage Hand had tore:
No daring *Negro* from the Bottom bore.
But th' o'rstock'd Soil, press'd with the too Rich Load,
Might send new *Colonies* abroad,
And Furnish all the Neighbouring Sea.
What boundless Riches in small space do ly;
When each one might a Province buy,
And Lavish *Cleopatra* feast and *Anthony*:

XIV.

Here *Marchasites* and unripe Mettals ly,
From the next Promontory rent,
By th' never sparing Sea:
Useless as yet,
The Precious Compounds want
The Sun's engendring Heat;
Which by kind Nature's Aid,
And Hatching Time, will once Mature be made,
And ly for Future Days a Bless'd Discovery.
The Artfull Salts, the *Chymists* use,
That Wonders can produce:

The

The Minerals, that have the Art
New Shapes to Mettals to impart,
And Monſtrous Changes cauſe
In ſpight of Nature's fixed Laws:
Th' Ingredients, that Compoſe
(If ſuch are unto Nature known)
The *Philoſophick* Stone,
Which Thirſty *Chymiſts* (that ſo Dote on gain,
They Broyl in the Devouring Fire in vain;
While all their Hopes in Empty Smoke do fly)
At any Value would obtain,
Would at an *Eaſtern* Kingdom's Purchaſe buy.---

XV.

There lies a Broken Anker, on whoſe Truſt
The Lives of all the Nautick Crew were Weigh'd;
That ſcarcely bore the firſt impetuous Guſt,
But Them to Rocks and Gaping Sands betray'd,
Or to the dreaded Strand:
There Heaps of Bodies under Hills of Sand,
(The *Mummies* of the Sea)
That at the *Reſurrection*-Day
Need take no Pains to make their Members hit,
Their Scatter'd Parts again to Knit;
But once inform'd with Heat and Active Fire,
Their Bodies will be found Entire,
And in one Moment be for *Riſing* fit.
Here *Guns* and *Swords* and Inſtruments of War,
That Death do give *near hand*, or from *afar*,
With thoſe, they ſlew, One Fortune ran:
Peaceably now they ly and *would* do ſo,
They of themſelves no Miſchief do,
Nor *would*, without the Cruel Hand of Man.

XVI.

There Two, that ſtrugling Sank into the Deep,
With Deadly Hate graſping Each Other faſt,

Ev'en Dead their Hostile Postures keep ;
The Enmity yet seems to last :
The senseless Bones Each Other hold,
Not Death th' unkind Embraces could unfold :
But when the Raging Tempests blow,
And Tydes move all the Deep below ;
The Clashing Bones yet seem to Jar,
And keep up a Perpetual War.----
Another lies hard by,
That o'rboard fell with a far-stretch'd-out Blow,
Aim'd at his Eager Foe,
And i'th' same Posture fell, i'th' same doth ly.
His Threatning Arm his Deadly Sword doth wield,
Menacing Death i'th' watry Field ;
And to Express His Ranker'd Hate within,
Dead He retains a Ghastly Grin.

XVII.

There Two in soft Embraces sleep ;
Death can't unclasp their folded Arms :
Love is a God above His reach,
Above His Injuries and Harms,
And even can Destiny Obedience teach :
They yet Love's Pleasures seem to reap,
Spight of Death's Adamantine Chain :
In spight of the great Change of Fate,
And all the Movings o'th' the unsetled Main,
A surly Billow bore *Her* into th' Sea,-----
Th' inflamed *Lover* could not stay behind,
But bid Defiance to the Wind,
And to th' Insulting Ocean's sway :
He leap'd into the Floud and caught
The Fatal Treasure in His Arms ;
Sunk with the Precious Weight,
Nor could refuse to die with that Dear Load of Charms.

'T

'Twas not a *Death* but *Extasie*!----
A tender Passion made Him grasp Her fast,
And He in Hopes of Safety was by Her embrac't.
Venus Her Self did the kind Lovers see,
(*Venus* her self sprang from the Sea ;)
And by Consent of all the Powers above,
Fix't it down a firm Decree ;
That from all Change and Injury free,
They should remain the Monuments of Love.
Their *Bodies* here below do Join,
Their Circling Limbs in Love-knots twine:
And i'th' *Elyzian* Shades (if we
May credit what's in other Regions done)
Their once-two *Souls* are now but One.----

XVIII.

There an Indulgent Mother lies,
Embracing yet Her tender Child :
With anxious thoughts She her fair Bosom fill'd,
For Her dear Infants Safety not Her own.
Minding more its Piercing Crys,
That did to Her the Storms and Tempests drown;
Than the Ship's confused Noise.
When Prudence bad Her Safety seek,
And every Soul did at the Danger schreek ;
She was singing Lullabies.
Her Head seems to'ward Her Child inclin'd,
Her Arms in tender Wreaths about it twin'd :
Upon its Cheeks Her Lips do rest,
And th' Infant yet doth seem to suck Her breast.

XIX.

To *Friendship's* Laws a Sacrifice,
In State a Gallant *Hero* lies,
And in His Death Himself doth seem to Pride.
When His Friend's Lift-up Hands did help implore,

When

When Gods were deaf unto a Wretches Prayer,
And Tempeſts roar'd ſo loud, they could not hear:
The ſide, which Heaven forſook,
With Generous Pride He took:
He Jump'd into the Foaming Tide,
And Him even from the Jaws of Ruine tore.
But Fate, that envy'd Him his Praiſe,
Put a Period to His Days;
Leſt He ſhould ſtop the Deſtiny's power.
Tyr'd with the ſaving of His Friend;
(So hard 'tis Strugling with our Fate)
The angry Sea th' Occaſion caught;
Commanded Tempeſts to attend,
And got a Worthleſs Victory
O'r One, that was half-dead before,
And yet o'r One, that cannot dy,
But in the Boſom of his Friend Survives;
And in the Book of *Fame* for ever Lives;
One ſtep alone on this ſide Immortality.

XX.

Here a Ship's Hulk, that many Storms had bore,
Viſited many a Diſtant Shore,
Enrich'd with *Eaſtern* and with *Weſtern* Store,
Now ſunk grows Richer, than it was before.
Oyſters, that Pearls breed in their Fruitfull Womb,
Do in her empty Cabbins ly:
Mountains of Golden Sand do for Her Ballaſt come,
And Amber-greaſe doth all the Hold employ.
Nothing to' enrich a Kingdom doth remain,
But once to make Her Tight and Fit to Sail again.

XXI.

There One, juſt ſinking in a Storm, yet ſtaid
To take with Him his God,
O'rwhelmed with the Precious Load,

S

A Quick-untimely Passage to the Bottom made.
In's Arms the Fatal Chest He yet doth hold,
Embraces, what his Ruine was, his Gold.
And what far more than Life was priz'd above,
Retains below unalterable Love.
Here Shatter'd Limbs and Scatter'd Treasures ly,
And never nearer come:
The Greedy Hand, that all did clasp,
Insatiably for more did roam,
Now senseless don't at Gold and Jewels grasp,
Which in his reach do lie,
Death nums the Covetous Hand and blinds the Greedy Eye.

XXII.

See there an once-Insatiate Head,
Ambitious, Covetous and Vain,
Whom never Bounds or Limits could contain!
Pearls stick his hollow Eye-holes full,
And Gold crams up his empty Skull.
And what alive He ne't could gain
By Fraud, by Prayers, or by Command,
He Purchases when Dead:
Even Rings (by th' working of the Sea)
Which the last Wrack became the Ocean's Prey,
Are Shuffled Artfully upon his hands:
That if his Covetous Soul could see
The State, in which He Dead doth ly,
She'd choose 't before a Life of Immortality.

XXIII.

There One, new-dead, becomes the Fishes prey,
And justling Crowds his Members gnaw;
His mangled Limbs around do draw.
Haddocks and *Codds* make Him their meat;
Lobsters and *Crabs* his Entrails eat,
And in his hollow Trunk their Eggs do lay.

And

And these by the next Fisher took,
By pleasing Bait and deadly Hook,
Become to Men luxurious food.
Men do Mankind in Fishes eat, and they
On Men revenge their near Relations blood.
A Mixture in our Nature is,
And the next step's a *Metempsychosis*.

XXIV.

There One, by Chance, or by kind Fate,
Entombed lay in so much state,
As might the Envy of the World create.
He was stretch'd out upon a *Pearly* Bed,
On sparkling Heaps of *Gold* his Head,
Branches of *Corall* round his Temples twind,
And like an artfull Shrowd his Limbs enshrind:
The *Fyllegrin* Case show'd all within,
And Studs of *Pearls* did at due distance shine.
No Mortal sure was ever laid
In so Magnificent, so rich a Room:
'Twas worth the Dying to have such a Tomb.----
A thousand Wonders more I did survey;
Round unregarded Heaps of Treasure lay
To every bold Adventurer a Prey;
But Fear still kept me in.-----
From far the precious Mountains shine,
And every daring Soul invite:
And oh! thought I, might I be Guide
To *English* Ships, that there might freight,
I could do more than *PHIPPS* and all his *Divers* did.

XXV.

By chance it was a solemn Day
Neptune made a Processive Round;
Rode in's Triumphal Chariot o'r the Sea
With Pride of all the *Ocean's* Beauties crownd.

'Twas in remembrance of the Time,
When he o'reburthen'd with the weight,
The Cares and Stings of his Imperial State,
When Hostile Robbers did his Realm infest,
Ravaged all the Watry Clime,
Broke up his Treasures in the *West*;
The richest Part of his Dominion,
That had to former Ages lain unknown;
When he in his own Court a Prisoner kept,
Durst not stir out for fear of Hostile Force:
But underneath th' *Atlantick* Island crept,
And in the hollow Ruines of her ancient Castles slept

XXVI.

In such Distress the watry God
Privately left his dark Aboad;
And under favour of the Night,
To Great *ELIZA's* Court did take his flight.
ELIZA, *Brittain's* thrice-Renowned Queen;
ELIZA, the Illustrious *Heroine*;
That Martial Spi it Patroniz'd his Cause,
And did assert his Injur'd Right.
Her tall Victorious Ships the Seas did scour,
Restor'd them to their Ancient Laws,
And Him unto his Native Power.
Great Soul! it was thy lucky Fate
The Sea and Land to vindicate:
Men to their Freedom to restore,
And Deities unto their Violated Power.
" To oblige *Kings* and Realms is Great,
" What then to put a *God* into thy Debt?

XXVII.

The Gratefull God the Favour own'd,
And that the Gift he might repay,
I'th' Sovereignty o'th' Sea
Her and Her Successors enthron'd:

And Yearly kept a Feaſt upon the happy Day.
The Noble Train near my *Aſylum* drew:
Neptune th' Auſpicious Place would ſee,
That once from dreaded Danger ſet him free.
My Transformation and my Fear he knew.
And, lifting up his awfull Trident High,
He ſmote the Face o'th' liquid Deep;
And charged all the watry Fry;
That they ſhould ſafely me from force and Rapine keep.

XXVIII.

Neptune ſate in his Chariot High
Drawn by Six *Hippopotami*;
Streamers of *Engliſh* Arms i'th' wanton Air did fly.
A Seagreen Robe was o'r his Shoulders ſpread,
Enrich'd with all th' unvaluable Store,
That Seas do breed or Storms devour:
And on his Head
A Crown of Rays from *Phœbus* ſent
Or as Acknowledgment, or Rent;
For Revelling each Night i'th' Deep,
For's hours of Paſtime or of Sleep.
On tunefull Shells the *Tritons* playd,
The Winds and Storms to ſleep were laid,
And a profound Peace o'r the Deep was ſpread.
Mermaids in melting ſtreins their Voices try'd,
And Sea-Nymphs in ſoft Airs reply'd;
That even rude Rocks & ſurly Seas took in the Muſick pride.

XXIX.

Mountainous *Whales* before the Court were ſent,
That mov'd all Lets out of the way;
And, where the Road thrô Creeks or Inlets lay,
Shuffled up Iſles into a Continent.
The Monſtrous *Norway-Whale* was one
That cover'd many Acres of the Sea;

That

That oft had for an Iſland gone,
Oft did the credulous Mariners betray,
Who moar'd their Ankers on his ſide,
And did beneath his Shelter ride.
Seas they drink down, and vomit up again;
And when they pleaſe do make an Ebb or Tyde;
Now 'tis Dry Land and now the Main.
Th' Aërial Beings (in a Fright)
That never ſince the Inundation
Such Cataracts of Seas had known,
Farther retir'd toward the Orbs of Light;
And fear'd the Loſs of their Dominion.
The troubled Sea around them boyls,
The Continent ſtartles, and the Iſles
For Fear ſhrink in their trembling Head;
And Earthquakes, as they turn their Courſe, are made.

XXX.

Near theſe their Place did take
Sea-Elephants that on the Rocks do ſleep,
That overlook the Deep;
Hang by the Teeth ſecure, nor wake,
Till treacherous Nets are ſet around,
Till they'r with Cords and Fetters bound,
Nor can one Struggle for their Freedom make.
The *Sea-Mors*, that's kill'd for his ſovereign Horn,
And thought by ſome the onely *Unicorn*.
The *Swordfiſh* and the *Thraſher*, that engage
The Monſter of the Sea;
And bloody Battels with the Whale do wage.
The *Tortoyſes*, that Barren Iſlands court,
From far to *Fruitleſs Sands* reſort,
And under them their Eggs do lay:
The *Dolphin*, that in Muſick doth delight,
And all ſurpaſſes in a ſpeedy Flight:

Porpoyſes

Porpoises, that make Storms their sport,
And only before Dangerous Tempests play:
The *Crocodile*, for Power and Cunning fam'd,
Nor for his Cruelty less Nam'd:
That Eats, and Weeps; that He may Eat again.
The *Shark*, an Enemy to Man,
That craftily about the Ships doth stay,
And never Spares his Prey:
Seales, that in hollow Caves delight,
And shun Man's Dangerous Sight,
On Barren Rocks and Isles are bred,
Where foot of Man did never tread.
The *Remora*, the Wonder of the Sea,
That Ships even under sail can stay:
Small in his Bulk, but hoisting round their Keels,
No Waves or Tydes the Captive force away:
Whom *Neptune* did forbid to touch his Chariot-wheels

XXXI.

Nor less those Swimmers added to the State,
That Earthly Creatures personate:
The *Lion*, *Bear*, and *Bull* o'th' Sea;
The *Horse* and *Hog*, that do i'th' Ocean play:
The long-bill'd Fish, to Birds of kin,
And that, which flyes with Moistned Fin.
The *Meremaid*, that doth Virgin Looks acquire,
The *Vayled Nunn* and *Cowled Fryer*;
Besides a Thousand Kinds, that have no Name,
That never to our Sight, or Knowledge came:
All, that their Castles on their Backs do bear,
All, that Offensive Weapons wear;
And all the Innocent Fry, that still to Death are near:
All, that Luxurious Palates please,
The Lustfull Dainties of the Seas;
All, that *Apicius* Table fit,
Or *Heliogabalus* with Joy would meet;

In Decent Order and with Comely State
Did on the Ceremony wait,
Nor did the Usefull *Herring* fail,
Whose Numerous Shoals ('tis said) can choke the *Whale.*

XXXII.

Thrice *Neptune* and his Court
With Mystick Rites and Songs of Joy
(While Milk-white Omens all around did fly)
Encompassed the *British* Isle,
And every River bless'd and every Port:
The *British* Isle! the best Beloved Seat
Of all the Off-spring of the Seas;
Whom He with Circling Arms doth ever greet.
And bad bless'd *Plenty*, *Victory*, and *Ease*
Upon her Charming Bosom smile:
Bad every Stream and every Rill
Plenty and Fruitfulness instill;
From *Thames*, that washes Stately Palaces,
Medway that Proud Victorious Navies sees,
To those that visit Humble Cottages.
Till all the whole Worlds Scatter'd good,
All, that's Esteem'd by th' Generous and Great,
Do in Her Lovely Bosom make aboad,
And there fix down their Glorious Shining Seat.
Till *England* be the Worlds Epitome:
And envy'd *Britannie*
The *Lesser World*, but yet the *Happier*, be.

A *PINDARIQUE* Ode.

PART. II.

STANZA. I.

THERE was an Isle, Fame sings,
To' Antiquity well known,
Whose Powerfull Kings
O'r *Africk* did extend their wide Dominion:
Th' *Atlantick* Island nam'd. ---- ----
West o'th' *Herculean* Straits the Happy Soil was spread,
With Arts and Arms Embellished,
With Peace and Justice Crown'd:
Till (many Ages long-since past)
Either that undermining Waves had tore
The unsecure Foundation;
Or Strugling Nature with the Burthen groan'd,
And Sunk beneath the Weight She bore;
Or Nature's God, for Crimes to Us unknown,
A Dreadfull Vengeance took,
And by an Earthquake's Power,
I'th' starting and affrighted Sea did sink Her down;
Earthquakes, that have the World's Foundation shook:
Have lowly Valleys into Mountains rais'd;
The Proudest Citties have debas'd,
And Towring Hills to Vales depress'd;
Old Isles overwhelm'd, and in their stead,
Made new Ones show their unknown head:

Heaven's unrelenting, all-devouring, Rod
The Dreadfull Messenger of Angry God.

II.

The Earth's Third Part sunk in one Moment down.----
The Guardian Angels were with Wonder strook;
Th' Infernal Shades th' Alarum took; (shook.
And th' other Parts o'th' World without an Earthquake
Even *Jove* and *Pluto*, Jealous grown,
Envied their Brother's late enlarg'd Dominion.
And all that *Western* Spacious Coast,
Which We *America* do stile,
Which was for many Ages lost
In dark Oblivion,
Beyond that Dangerous Ocean spread,
E'r Great *Columbus* his Discovery made;
Prov'd but some small remains of that most Potent *Isle*.

III.

Hither Great *Neptune's* Course did lead
To th' Palace o'th' *Atlantian* Kings:
Which doth the wildest thoughts exceed,
Castalian Fury e'r did breed,
Which *Bacchanals* or *Dithyrambiques* sings:
Outdoes those Notions, fill the Poet's head,
When *Pegasus* expands his Wings:
More Rich, more Stately, and more Bright,
Than all, that heated Rage can write;
All, that Flattery can indite:
All, that Inventive *Greece* did once bestow,
On Gods above, or on their Kings below:
The *Fabrick* did more Excellencies shew,
Than e'r from Poet's Fancy were instill'd;
" Thô they can Richest, Quickest, and the Cheapest build.

IV.

Here in a Spacious Hall,
A Faithfull Register was kept of all

The

The memorable Conquests of the Sea:
E'r since the Universal Floud, when She
Her Empire over all had hurl'd,
And *Neptune* rul'd the World.
What her old Limits were before;
Where She unchang'd doth keep
The Bounds of Lands and of the Deep.
Where th' *Ocean* doth usurp upon the shore;
And where the Land possesses, what She had.
Where Hills were by the Deluge made,
Where Continents broke, and Isles were spread
And where, what once was Sea, now Land appears:
Charts of the Land and Sea, as once it stood,
Before the Changes of the Sweeping *Floud*;
And as it now is Seen to later Years.

V.

The Voyage of the Heaven-contrived Ark,
Which Providence did safely Steer;
While She, th' whole Species did of Mankind bear:
The first frail Bark,
In which Men durst attempt to trust the Sea!
The Minutes kept, how every Day
Her Sacred Course thrô th' Ocean lay:
When She to *East* or *West* did Steer,
When She to *North* or *South* did bear:
When She o'r *Europe* sail'd, or *Asia*;
And how Mount *Ararat* at last Her Course did stay.

VI.

The certain time, when by Impetuous Rage,
The Great *Atlantian* State sank down;
And did the Sea-Gods Temples Crown;
Six Centuries before great *Plato's* Age:

When *Sicily* from *Calabria* was rent,
And when beloved *Brittain* from the Continent.
When *Goodwin* Sands
Was once a Powerfull Prince's Lands.
When *Ægypt's* Fruitfull Soil
Was ravish'd from the Sea by Mud and Filth of *Nile*.
When th' Ocean shall new Conquests make,
When, what did once belong to Her, retake.
When *Holland* must Her Debts repay,
And count for all Her Provinces stole from the Sea.
He that would Curious be,
And know of future Times the Destiny,
He need but Visit that Great Court and see.

VII.

There in another Column stood,
The Great Commanders of the Floud:
Those that have uncontrouled swept the Seas,
And Triumph'd o'r the Watry Provinces.
When the Sea Infant-Burthens bore,
And Men sail'd Safe in sight of shore,
Nor trusted to the Wind but to the Oar.
When Daring Men by Custom Bolder made,
But by Experience more,
With heavy Fleets the Ocean did invade.
When bold *Phœnicia* could not stay at home,
But did for Gain to distant Regions roam:
Did Rich *Atlantis* rape,
Nor could our *CASSITERIDES* Escape.
When Purple *Tyre* sate Mistress of the Sea:
When *Carthage* rais'd her Emulous Head,
And o'r Imperial *Rome* prevail'd;
When her Bold Fleets the Ocean's Bosom spread,
And *Hanno* first of all round *Africk* sail'd:

When

When *Greece* from them the Secret got,
And *Alexander*, that both Empires sought,
Sail'd by *Nearchus* unto *India.*
When *Rome* to her own Coast confin'd
Dar'd not to trust the faithless Wind:
Till from some Ships wreck'd on the Shore
She learnt the Dangerous trade;
And grew so' expert her Neighbours to invade:
And made th' unquiet World the fatal Skill deplore.

VIII.

When with the *Roman* Empire Arts too dy'd;
And Barbarous Rage took in the Downfall pride.
When Fear and dire Necessity
Compell'd the frighted Troops, that fled,
Inhospitable Cliffs to choose,
Secure from Reach of Barbarous Foes:
Whence *Venice* rais'd her glorious Head;
Venice, the Jewel of the Sea;
With silver Feet that on the Waves doth tread,
But her high Temples among Stars doth lay.
When the great Secret of the *Loadstone* found
For bold Discoveries gave a ground:
That doth thro pitchy Night and Darkness guide,
Miraculously finds the unseen Way,
When there's no Marks nor Tracts left in the liquid Sea,
Even when the Polestar's hid.

IX.

When *English* Ships with gallant Pride
Did o'r the subject Sea in Triumph ride.
And all the Men, that Former times did grace,
The *Heroes* of Immortal Race,
All, whose brave Souls with Valour were inflam'd,
All, that for Arts or Arms were nam'd,
For Victories on Land or Sea were fam'd;

Seem'd

Seem'd by a *Metempsychosis*
In *Englishmen* again to rise.
When all, that Ancient *Greece* dar'd doe,
Or *Tyre* or *Carthage* skill could know,
Or *Rome's* exalted Minds could show ;
Or later *Venice*, that Espous'd the Sea,
Are all compriz'd in Our one *Brittany*.

X.

Around hung the surprizing Sights
Of all the Memorable Fights,
That ever dy'd with Gore the frighted Main:
Where Art with Nature for the Empire strove ;
The Ships yet seem'd to move,
The Men to live,
Their Former Rage and Vigor to retain :
Their swollen Limbs did bold Defiance breathe
And gave a Life to Death :
Their blood shot Eyes yet darted Fire,
And their stretch'd Veins did show their inward Ire.
The Draughts of Wars in Ages long-since gone
Lapp'd up in dark Oblivion ;
To which no tracts nor Footsteps lead
But even the very Fame is dead :
In lively Portraytures are shown,
In Postures and in Garbs are drawn,
To Us and all the World unknown.
There *Maps* of Realms, whereof we ne'er did hear,
That lie Rewards for future Industry ;
Whose very Names yet never reach'd our Ear,
But to succeeding Times shall be familiar.
That might we thence Great *Neptune's* Records bear,
And all the Secrets of his Court declare,
How welcome to the Inquisitive World would such an Histo-
(ry be!

XI. The

XI.

The Memorable Time was set
When *Xerxes* did the Ocean beat,
And fetter'd up the *Hellespont* :
Which unrevenged long bore not th' Affront.
When He, his Numerous Army by an Handfull torn,
His Bridge of Boats by Tempests overborn,
In a poor Schiff was forc'd to pass that Sea,
Which he once bragg'd, He'd taught to' obey
The former Feats of ancient *Greece*,
Ever since *Jason* won the Golden Fleece.
What they have told in Vanity and Pride,
What they've forgot and what they've magnify'd ;
Where they've told Truth, and where they've ly'd.

XII.

The Struggle, *Carthage* made, to try,
When just expiring, for her Liberty :
When yielding to inevitable Fate
She sunk unwillingly beneath the weight :
When all her Beauteous Ladies deign'd to spare,
To make new Cordage for her Ships, their Hair.
Nor was forgot
The bloody Battle, that was fought,
When *Carthage* lofty Head was low,
With *Hannibal Rome's* Mortal Foe,
That Barrel'd Vipers into *Roman* Ships did throw.

XIII.

There was describ'd at large
The great Deciding Fight,
That to the Empire of the World did give the Victor Right.
There *Cleopatra's* Gilded Barge
With curious Workmanship did shine,
And promis'd something Great within.

With

With base ignoble Fear she fled ;
The gallant Warriour turn'd his Head,
His Head and Heart with Her was led.
With her loose Charms betray'd
He could not stay behind,
Weak and Effeminate as Woman-kind ;
He could not want her Look,
His mighty Heart in pieces broke :
Honour and Fame forgot,
The Empire of the World esteem'd at nought,
He turn'd his Sails and said ;
" In Empire I have had my share,
" Gallant my Acts have been in War,
" And I in Love as nobly dare.
" I can't thy Presence, *Cleopatra*, lose,
" The World for Thee I'l give :
" And rather now to be thy Captive choose
" Than the World's Emperour live.
So He with Love, not Fear o'recome,
" Follow'd his Heart and left to *Cæsar Rome*.

XIV.

There *Pompey's* Gallant Sons were shown
Crowned with Honour and Renown.
The Noblest Spirits, *Rome* e'r bore,
Who influenc'd with Generous Rage
Both for a violated Country's Good,
And for a Murder'd Father's Blood,
Did against *Cæsar* and the World engage ;
And first did learn the Ocean to command the Shore.
Nor was thrô all the Ages down
A memorable Action pass'd,
When *Rome* retain'd her old Renown,
Or when with Barbarous Rage her Glory was defac'd ;
Till Fam'd *Lepanto's* happy Fight,
That did the Sea of *Turkish* Force acquit.

XV. Ther

XV.

There was the * Famous Sea-Fight ſhown,
Which unto *Scluce* did give ſo vaſt Renown,
Scluce, in the Books of Fame well-known!
Nor *Greece* from *Salamis* did bear
A Richer Prize, than *Albion* purchas'd there:
When our *Third* *EDWARD* and his Godlike Son,
The Admir'd *BLACK-PRINCE*, did raiſe the *Engliſh* Name,
And proud *Valois* his Mighty Fleet o'recame,
Aſſerting o're the Seas their high Dominion.
The Feathered Meſſengers of Fate
Flew thick, as ſtorms of Hail, from *Engliſh* Bows:
Nor could the *French* endure their ſtinging Weight,
But rather deſparately Choſe
Their gaping Wounds in the ſalt Floods to cloſe.
Then thrice-ten thouſand *French* their Lives reſign'd,
Staining the *Brittiſh* Seas with hoſtile Gore;
Their fainting *Lillies* now grew ſick and pin'd;
While *Neptune* trembled at our Angry *Lyon's* Roar.

* *Battle* of Scluce near Flanders. *A. D.* 1340.

XVI.

But above all with greateſt Care,
(For leſſer Fights are loſt,
As ſmaller Sounds are by the Great ingroſt)
The Wonder and the Scorn o'th' Sea,
That even frighted the ſubmiſſive Eye,
The Great *Armada*, ſwell'd with *Spaniſh* Pride,
That came to take Poſſeſſion, not to War,
Was in moſt coſtly Colours drawn,
Did in Triumphant Manner ride,
Already ſure of Victory;
Had *England* in vain Hopes already ſwallow'd down.
Till *Engliſh* Valour thrô the empty ſhadows broke
The Pompous Fleet in pieces ſhook;
Th' unweildy Carracks gôt new wings to fly.

U The

The *Burthens* of the Sea
Did *Burthens* now unto themſelves become;
And wiſh'd, they could ſhrink into leſſer Room.
Their Fetters and their Chains were took,
And even their Inſtruments of Cruelty
Did to their Owners dreadfull look;
And told what was their Doom:
Thrô all the *Northern* World they fled;
Each Promontory did their Treaſure ſhare;
Each barren Soil enriched by the War:
Beyond the Fartheſt *Thule* trembling and agaſt,
They by their Valiant Foes were chac't:
And Famine, Cold and Ignominy paſt,
The poor Remains reel'd ſhatter'd and deſpiſed Home at laſt.

XVII.

Nor did the skilfull Art omit
The Acts in various Ages done,
That eve'n did Fame affright;
Which no bold Language could recite,
Nor could by Pencil's skill be drawn.
All Species of Ships were there,
Thoſe, that firſt cut the Waves with Fear;
And near the Shore did creep:
Thoſe, that with Oars did laſh the Deep;
Thoſe, whoſe wide Sails the Waves did ſweep:
From the tall Flagg-ſhip, Pride of all the Main,
To the Canoo o'th' Sun-burnt *Indian.*

XVIII.

And, as a ſign of Confidence, was ſhow'd
The Secret Book,
In which no one but Favourites may look,
Nor even are thoſe allow'd;
Till Sanctions bid them Secrets keep
Nor e'r reveal the Myſteries o'th' Deep.

There

There were large Charts o'th' *Southern* unknown Land,
How the Coaſt trends to *Eaſt* and *Weſt*.
In what Degrees of Longitude 'tis laid,
How far to th' *Southern* Pole 'tis ſpread.
The Capes and Promontories were expreſs'd,
Where a Safe Port, and where a Dangerous Strand;
Where Ships ſecure may ride, and where lies hid a Sand.
The Depth of Rivers and of Shores were took,
Not even a Creek, but was mark'd down:
The Traffick, Strength, and Riches of each Town,
That on the Neighbouring Sea doth look.
Their Cuſtoms both in Peace and War,
What Merchandize the Land doth bear:
What they do want, and what they ſpare.
The Trade-winds, that do thither blow,
The Roads, that thither lead.
And Iſles, that are i'th' Paſſage ſpread:
That He, who the leaſt Skill doth know,
May thither without help o'th' Compaſs go.

XIX.

There, what hath puzled Curious Brains,
But ne r Rewarded for the Coſt or Pains,
Are Maps, that do diſplay
The *Northern* Paſſage to *Cathay*.
Where the Strait opens, and where ly
The Sea-marks for Diſcovery;
How to 'ſcape broaken Lands, that there ariſe,
And how to' avoid the Shoales of Ice:
VVhere the Coaſt *Southward* bends,
And where the *Scythic* Promontory ends.
Th' extent of *BACON'S Polar* Land,
Charts of the Doleſull Strand;
The Icy Mountains, that affright:
How the Inhabitants the rigid cold do bear,

And misty Damps of the condensed Air,
How they endure an half-year Night.
Besides the Virgin Soils, that never yet
Did Conquest or Discovery admit;
That in his secret Catalogue are writ.

XX.

Nor were the Secrets of his Empire hid,
Where the fam'd Rivers (*Paradice's* Pride)
Whose Names and Scituation
With endless Contests have Mens Brains employ'd,
Yet in their wanted Channels run;
And like *Seth's* Pillars have surviv'd the Flood.
Where Isles, that have from the Creation stood,
By restless Waves are undermin'd,
And with next Earthquake will a Ruine find.
Where Infant growing Isles do swell,
And will in future Times their Heads reveal.
Where old *Phœnician* Wracks have slept,
Treasures from former Ages kept:
Stores, that would be
Priz'd for their Worth and more for their Antiquity.
Who shall in future Ages rule the Sea,
And Acts of Ancient Times outdoe.
The Fortune and the Fate of *Brittanie*,
When the Espoused Sea shall *Venice* leave,
And Her of all Her pristin Fame bereave;
A certain Symptom of approaching Woe.
And what hath unto Ages lain unknown,
There is an Art the Longitude to find:
And, what don't less Distract the Curious Mind,
The Reason of the Needle's *Variation*.

XXI.

There one might know
The Fate of every One, that unto Sea doth go:

What

What Prosperous Winds shall Him attend,
What Lucky Adventures Him befriend,
Or if unruly Storms his Shatter'd Bark shall rend.
Where controverted *Ophir* lyes,
Whence *Solomon* had his Rich Supplies.
Where th' floating Isle, the *Proteus* of the Sea,
Obeys Great *Neptune's* Law,
And doth a fixed Mansion get.
Where Polar Loadstone Isles are set,
(If any such there be)
That the touch'd Needle draw.
Where working Seas shall Harbors fill,
And Towns of Trade
Shall shrink to Villages from their Exalted State ;
And in their stead
Some Despicable Place grow Great.

XXII.

This Palace once th' *Atlantian* Kings did own,
In its own Structure Beauteous 'twas and Great:
But all its former Glories are outdone,
By Juices which do ly to us unknown,
Such as do Gems and Precious Stones beget :
And by the Plastick Power which Nature secret keeps,
But in dark Mines reveals, and i'th' unfathom'd Deeps ;
By these her Structures all are turn'd to *Adamant*,
And neither Darling Beauty nor unyielding Hardness want.
Unviolated Temples stand,
That don't beneath Time's burthen groan :
Neither by Tydes nor Storms bore down,
Nor Injured by rowling Sand.
Branches of winding *Corall* crawl
Upon the Sacred Wall,
Like clasping Ivy round embrac't :
Which never Sacrilegious Hand
Or Savage Force defac'd.

Th' Al-

Th' Altars within their Privileges retain,
Do Sanctuaries yet remain:
Thither the helpless Fry
Pursu'd by Violence do fly,
And from th' *Asylum* all their Foes defy.
They to the Helpless yet do lend their Aid,
Nor may Arm'd Force the Sacred Seats invade.

XXIII.

Within and round are shown
The Tombs of the *Atlantian* Kings;
Which of themselves are Stately things,
But by accession of Sea-Treasure Nobler grown.
Each common Stone
A *Jaspis* or an *Hyacinth* doth grow:
Mother of *Pearl* the common roads doth strow,
And ev'n *Plebean* Tombs do *Sapphires* show.
And He, who last did in *Atlantis* Reign,
That to futurity he might remain,
Beyond the common doom,
Which swallows up the Worthless Crowd,
Neptune on Him his Greatest Gem bestow'd,
A Gem so Great, it serv'd Him for a Tomb.
There Queens in *Chrystall* Monuments were set,
That show'd the Beauty lay within:
Who from themselves much Fame did get;
But from what th' Ocean lent did seem Divine.
Some did in Tombs of *Amber* live,
And nothing to a Life did want, but Breath:
A Grave more Precious and more Fair,
Than all *Arabia's* Gums could give:
Than *Ægypt* for Her Monarchs did prepare,
Or *Artemisia* did to Her Dear Lord bequeath.

XXIV.

The Princely Gardens kept their Beauteous Store;
With Powdred *Pearls* the Walks were ſpread,
Nor is upon Earth's Boſom bred
A Beauteous Flower,
But by kind Nature's Artfull power
The ſame of Precious Jewels there was made,
Which no Time ever can devour.
Cloſe Arbors and aſpiring Groves,
That were intruſted oft with ſecret Loves,
By Petrifying Juice are turn'd to Stone:
And the ſame Order and Proportion
They yet unchanged own.
Deſigned Wracks the Treaſuries do ſtore
With rarities of every diſtant ſhore:
The Noted Ports yet Ships do ſhow,
Whom Tempeſts overbore;
And order'd ſo
That they into the very Harbors fell:
And Bloody Sea-fights do the uſeleſs Armories ſwell.

XXV.

A Band of *Triton's* upon *Neptune* wait,
And Guard his Palace Gate,
And yet keep up the old *Atlantian* State.
The Caſtles and the Towns remain,
The Citties yet their Privileges retain:
Tritons do in the Nobles Houſes ſtay,
And Sea-Nymphs in the Groves and Meadows play.
On Earth Viciſſitude of Things
Rules o'r the Peaſants Spade and Crowns of Kings,
Citties are not exempt from Fate,
But, as they had their Birth, ſhall have their Date.
Their Names and Scituation ſoon are loſt;

And

And She, whose lofty Head stood high,
In the next Age in lowly Dust shall lie,
And even her very Ruines be forgot.
But here *Atlantis* doth a Conquest boast,
Which i'th' uncertain Sea
Hath from all Change Exemption got,
And's plac'd beyond the Reach of Destiny.

A *PINDARIQUE* Ode.

PART III.

STANZA I.

HEnce Curiosity me led
To view the Neighbouring Sea:
Where 'tis with Green *Sargossa* spread,
And imitates a Flowry Mead;
Doth the unwearied Eye to rove invite,
And every where gives Prospects of Delight:
Under whose Shade the harmless Fry,
No Fear nor Danger nigh,
Their Innocent Revels keep,
And deck with sparkling Pearly scales the Deep.
Where *Tortoyses* from far resort,
Journy again unto their well-known Port;
Do with unwearied Feet repair
Unto the Place, where they were bred,
Or where before their Eggs they laid;
And without Guide, but Nature being their Friend,
Thrô devious ways are without Pole-star led:
And upon barren Desolate Isles,
They stupidly unto the Care
Of Hatching Sands their shelly Brood commend,
Or to the Sun's auspicious Smiles.

II.

Where Artfull *Crabs*, by Nature taught,
Their Food of *Oysters* and of *Muscles* make:

Whose Armory of Shells so well is wrought,
Their furious Gripes can't the Contexture break.
But when to take in pearly Dew they o'pe,
The watchfull *Crabb* doth the Occasion steal,
With little Stones the gaping Shells doth fill;
That those on whom rude Force could nought avail,
By Policy are caught.
Where the poor Fish, to all a Prey,
On whom kind Nature hath bestow'd
An Art to raise himself above the Flood,
Doth his useless Skill essay.
By *Albicores* and *Dolphins* he pursued
With moistned Fin knows how to fly,
But can't avoid his steady Destiny.
Sea-Fowl his Course prevent,
Seize on the helpless Prey:
And he, that durst not trust the Sea,
Dies in a Foreign Element.
A sad *Dilemma*, when to stay or fly,
Death equally is nigh:
Death that doth to all Seats repair,
That neither Land nor Sea doth spare,
Nor the swift Flights of those, that cut the Air.

III.

Nor did I miss the Plain,
Where the Seas Terrour, the *Leviathan*,
In his extended Pride doth reign.
Whose Subjects do at awfull Distance wait,
And dread him as their Fate.
But not his Monstrous Bulk and Mighty State,
Not his devouring Jaws
Can stop his Destiny;
Such often is the Doom of High and Great,
Such are Fate's rigid Laws,

By despicable Foes to die.
So scorned Vapours oft the Earth have shook:
So Worms destroy the aged Oak,
Neither by Tempest nor by Thunder strook:
So *Elephants* despised *Mice* do kill,
So the *Ægyptian Rat* the sleeping *Crocodile*.

IV.

Two Fish, but small in Bulk, yet great in Mind,
When none the mighty Monster dare assail,
With Skill and Force combin'd
Revenge their murder'd Kind;
One arm'd with Sword, the other with a Flail.
This from below th' unweildy Monster gores,
Nor can he to his Deeps descend:
The other furious Blows upon him showers,
From which no Armour can defend.
Which way soe'r he moves he finds his Doom;
The goring Sword, if he descends, he meets,
And furious Batteries; if he up doth come:
Death on each Weapon waits;
No way is left to fly,
But, while his trembling Subjects wait th' Event,
He meets his uncontrouled Destiny.
And what doth aggravate his Fall, he dies
Not by an Equal Combatant,
But those he did despise!

V.

Nor did I miss to' enquire
What symptoms in the Sea were seen,
Before a Storm doth rise,
While all is yet serene;
What Ebullitions are i'th' Ocean made,
While nothing doth our Eyes or Ears surprize.
What secret skill by Nature is convey'd

To *Sea-fowls*, that to Isles retire ;
And *Porpoyses*, that they
Only before the Tempests play :
How they those Secrets know,
Which strange to Men do show.
When Storms the troubled Waters shall molest,
When Calms shall Lap the Sea in rest ;
And how the *Halcyon* knows when to prepare her Nest.

VI.

Where in dark Caves
That do no Rays admit,
Beneath the Force of foaming Waves,
And Influence of Cheerfull Light,
The ragged *Sea-Calves* make a Safe Retreat.
Where they in solitary Holds do breed,
And gloomy Seats and Safety do prefer,
To all the Pompous Shows that Danger bear :
And where with Milky Breasts the *Seales* their Young Ones (feed.

VII.

How rising *Spouts*, the Wonders of the Sea,
Or drawn by th' Sun's attractive heat,
Or rarified by Subterranean fire,
Do in Ætherial Regions play ;
And mix with Seas above the Firmament.
How they new Qualities do get,
And against Nature's Laws aspire :
And from their Kindred Waters rent
Do revel in the Air ;
That's now become a Watry Plain.
How the Vast Pillar doth the Burthen bear,
And gives new Nourishment for Clouds and Rain.
How frighted Mariners, when nigh,
VVith spread-out Sails the Danger shun ;

The

The Dreadfull Neighbourhood do fly,
Which on what e'r it falls doth drown.

VIII.

Nor did the Dreadfull Gulph my Voyage ſtay,
That ope's a Paſſage to th' *Pacifick* Sea:
Whether by the Great *Workman's* hand 'twas made
For Commerce and Enriching Trade:
Or whether reſtleſs Waves the way had tore
On the Vaſt Chaſm, was rent with Earthquake's power;
It lyes th' amazing way into another World.
Th' unfathomable *Depths* appall:
The Waves in Dreadfull *Storms* are ever curl'd,
In *Hurricanes* and *Whirlwinds* furl'd.
The unrelenting *Cliffs* do never ſave,
And the Vaſt *Chaſm* doth repreſent a Grave.
The hanging *Rocks*, that threat a fall,
The foaming *Waves*, that rage below,
And *Hills* above all cloath'd with Snow,
That rob the Gulph of half the Day,
And hide the Sun's Auſpicious Ray;
The furious *Winds* that from the Mountains break,
And headlong *Guſts*, that Ships in pieces ſhake;
Th' *Abyſs*, that doth no Light admit,
But ſeems for Fiends a dark Retreat;
The *Rocks*, on which no Peace doth ſit;
The *Shores*, that do no food or ſhelter ſhow,
And *Savages*, that do no Pitty know:
Fiercer than Rocks, and Ruder than the Wind,
A Dreadfull Scene preſent unto the Trembling Mind.

IX.

Nor leſs the *Northern* Seas my Courſe invite,
Doubly fenc'd by Ice and Night.
Where Nature's fixed Bars are laid,
The Fetters nothing can invade,

But

But Heavenly heat from the Sun's presence shed,
Where the unfathomable Depths are spread :
Where Ghastly Horrour and Confusion dwell,
Gloomy, Dark, and Deep, as Hell :
Whose Stranger Waves ne'r bore the Plowing Keel,
Nor e'r the Lashes of the Oar did Feel ;
Nor were Discover'd, but by Thee,
Generous and much-Lamented *Willoughby* !

X.

Where Barren Isles exalt their Head,
Uncomfortable, as the Seas ; in which they'r spread
Whose Hoary Heads, cloath'd with Eternal Snow,
No Friendship with the Sun do know ;
But all in Icy Fetters bound remain :
Congeal'd in Numerous Centuries slid by,
The Streams a Chrystal hardness gain,
So Hard, they never will relent :
But when the World a Sacrifice shall dy,
And in her Funeral Flames expire,
They shall outbrave the Raving Element ;
Nor yield to that, which Conquers all things, Fire.

XI.

Where the Bold Savage doth ill Fate defie ;
The force of Storms and Mounting Seas outbraves,
And safely Dances on the Threatning Waves,
And truly may be said to rule the Sea.
Clos'd in his Boat secure He rows,
Made of the Skins of Fish, He took his Prey ;
Which, by a secret Sympathy,
Do with the well-acquainted Waves agree,
And in a lasting Friendship close.
Lock'd in his Schiff they can't a Passage find,
Nor one Inquisitive Drop can search a way :
Thô Water doth thrô Rocks and Mountains wind,

And in each Particle of Matter ly.
Antiquity of *Centaurs* told,
That did half-Men, half-Horſes grow;
The Fumes of wild Poetick Heads of Old.
A ſtranger Wonder He doth ſhow
A Man (if yet a *Man*) above, a Monſter all below
In *Scales*-skins cloath'd He doth the Fiſh deceive,
Who Him one of their Shoal believe,
Untill his Fatal Dart
Credulity's Reward to them doth give:
He Perſonates a Fiſh with ſo much Art,
That not their piercing Eye,
Thô ſight in them in its Perfection be,
And doth, what they in other Sences want, ſupply
Can any difference ſpy.
He lives, He eats, He ſleeps i'th' Sea,
Which ſeems to be his Element,
And gives that Food, the Barren Shores deny;
And doth his Bed, his Drink, his Sport preſent:
And it a Queſtion yet remains,
What Claſſis of the Creatures He is in,
Whether He is to Men or Fiſh of Kin:
Whether He more to Earth or Sea doth owe,
To th' Solid or the Liquid Plaines,
And if what doth his Food beſtow,
May not be thought his Mother too:
If that, which doth his Wants relieve,
Mayn't be ſuppos'd his *Being* firſt to give.

XII.

Neceſſity doth teach Him Art;
And thô the Soil's to Him unkind,
And doth all Needfull Inſtruments deny,
His Sport, what e'r He needeth, doth impart:
For by kind Nature's Aid He all in's Prey doth find.

Of Fishes Fins his Boat is made,
And with their Skins 'tis overspread,
Their Bones the room of Hooks supply,
And from their Teeth He forms his deadly Dart.
A Circling Pleasure that hath never End,
Doth on his Quiet Life attend.
Full Shoals of Fish to Him resort,
Who by their Death to others Death bequeath,
They with them bring the Instruments of Death,
And by their Own do Ruine unto Others give;
And He can ne'r want Tackle, if He hath but Sport
Alive Great Fish do on the Lesser feed,
Do Ravin even on those they breed:
Here, when they'r dead, the Enmity doth live;
They senseless do become their Enemies Bane,
And after Death a Conquest over others gain.

XIII.

Nor did I miss, by Inclination led,
(For 'tis an Art my Soul doth please)
To visit all the Spacious Fruitfull Seas,
That are with Numerous Shoals of Fishes spread.
Where they upon the Artist wait,
With Greedy Hast swallow the Deadly Bait,
And Quarrel, who the first shall meet their Fate.
By Ill Example led they still rush on,
Regardless of their Friend's Destruction:
Whose Mangled Parts their Hungry Jaws do eat,
That now are dress'd up for their meat,
And made the Engines of Deceit.
Unhappy Case! where Fellows Traytors are,
And where Society becomes a Snare!
Where Death to th' Living no Advice doth give,
And where Dead Friends the Living do decieve!

From hence with winged ſpeed I fled,
Did all around as Enemies dread:
And where no warning was from Ruine took,
Did on my ſelf as on a Traytor look.

XIV.

I ſaw, where floating Woods of Timber, rent
From th' undermined Continent,
By *Northern* Tempeſts furious blow;
Or elſe o'recharg'd by weight of Ice and Snow,
As hanging on the Cliffs they grow,
They break, and into th' ſubject Sea do glide:
How they in unknown Paths their Journeys ſteer,
Till wakefull Providence's Care,
That Neceſſaries doth for all provide,
Their Courſe to barren Iſles doth guide,
Which, by th' Inclemency of their raw Air,
Never a Tree or Shrub did bear,
But the Inhabitants in want do to the' Sea repair.
Their Darts and Bows to Waves they owe,
Their Houſes do from Tempeſts grow:
Their Food they draw from Tydes;
And their cold frozen Sea their uſefull Fire provides.

XV.

I ſaw the *Sea-Mors* chac'd, whoſe prized Horn
That doth his fatal Head adorn
His Deſtiny doth bequeath,
And what's deſign'd his Safety, proves his Death:
Where Iſles of Ice, remote from any Shore,
Themſelves at eighty Fathom moar:
Look like a Continent,
And Capes and Cliffs, and Promontories repreſent.
Upon whoſe Tops wild Beaſts do fight,
And Sea-fowls make the Cliffs look doubly white.

XVI.

Nor here my Curiosity was ſtaid,
But with bold Courſe my daring Eyes ſurvey'd
Where ſecret Paſſages o'th' Deep were laid.
Where by the working of the Sea,
Or by ſome ſecret Cauſe to us unknown;
The winding waters find their hidden way:
And ſtraining thrô the Earth do leave behind
The Saltneſs, they did from their Mother own,
Till fit for Uſe, Delight, and Nouriſhment, they'r grown.
And on ſome Mountain's ſide
They do a Paſſage find:
Thrô flowiy Meadows wind,
Thrô fruitfull Valleys glide
Till they i'th' Sea again do their Ennobled Waters hide.

XVII.

Nor did I fear
Beneath ſtupendious Rocks my Courſe to ſteer;
The hidden Tracts and lonely Vaults to' explore,
That under Mighty Realms do ſink,
Thrô which the thirſty *Caſpian*,
The *CASPIAN*, that doth numerous Rivers drink,
Yet ſtill unſatisfi'd doth gape for more,
Nor ever ſwells with all the Store,
Empties it ſelf into th' *Mediterranean*.
I did not fear the headlong Gulf, which all
The Mariners its *Navel* call:
The *Vortex*, which the Sea drinks down,
And all, that comes within its Verge, doth drown.

XVIII.

Nor to my Curious Search did ſecret lie
The devious Ways in Regions deep below,
That do 'twixt diſtant *Lakes* and *Oceans* go.

Ho

How the Friendly Waters meet,
How the Shoals of Fishes greet
In Realms yet undiscover'd to the Eye.
How *Meers*, whose Heads and Springs we cannot see,
Nor what their Sourse doth breed,
An Entercourse do keep
With Caverns under Mountains laid,
Or with the Treasures of the Deep:
How what the Sea doth from the Land receive,
When swelling Rivers to her Bosom come,
She back again in Springs and Showers doth give,
And keeps an *Æquilibrium*.

XIX.

There lies a Deep, if we may Truth receive
From those, that on the Seas do live,
Not far from th' *CAPE*, that hath a Name from *Hope*,
Where no Art can a Bottom gain;
Thô they a thousand Fathom sound with Rope,
But all their Labour and their Charge is vain.
Here I sunk down into the deep Abyss,
Where no created Being e're before
The Secrets went to' explore,
Or Nature's Work, that near the Center lies.
Below vast Rocks and massy Mounts I past,
Such as the Upper World don't know;
The Strength and Fortresses below,
On which the World is plac'd:
Till thrô dark Paths and uncut Ways,
Being arriv'd at th' utmost Place,
Where ev'en sharp Thoughts could not a farther passage (trace;
I my wearied Journey staid
At *Natures* Bars, by the Almighty made.

XX.

The Bars, that fence the Windows of the Deep,
The raging Waves secure;
Lest they again the Earth should sweep,
And all Mankind devour.
But who the wondrous Locks can tell
VVho can the *Adamantine* Gates reveal?
That fortifie the firm Decree,
Which hath forbid the Ocean to rebell,
Set Limits to the Imperious Sea,
And made her in her Confines dwell.
Here I in vain for *Dæmogorgon* sought,
The Monster, ancient Ages thought,
Did at the *Center* lie;
The VVorld did actuate;
Whose Breath did make the Seas with Tydes to swell,
And whose unruly Motion Earthquakes did create.

XXI.

Now thrô dark subterranean Caverns led
And solitary Roads below;
Upon whose Brow sits dismal Night,
VVhere massy Rocks exclude the Light;
VVhere ghastly Horrour and Distraction's laid.
Led by Instinct, not by Sight,
VVhere *Zembre's* Lake doth fruitfull Waters show,
The wish'd-for Light I do regain,
And what Antiquity did never know
Find *Nile's* Illustrious Head.
Down all his glorious Course I cut my Way,
Thrô all the Realms that do his Waves adore;
The thirsty Nations that his Help implore:
Not the steep *Cataracts* could force my stay,
VVhose dreadfull Downfall doth the Sight surprize,
And dulls the *Eye*, as th' *Ear* is deafned with the Noise

My daring Course with them I downward led,
Nor fear'd the Treacherous *Crocodile*,
Nor *Hippopotamus* of *Nile*:
View'd the remains of Dark Antiquity,
Wept o'r its Pristin Glory fled,
And griev'd to see the Marks of present Slavery.

XXII.

Nor did the *Jewish* Sea,
Fill'd with *Bitumen* 'scape Discoverie:
Trembling I at its Borders stood,
But durst not trust the Poys'nous Flood.
No Creature can the Noxious Waves abide,
Nothing can thrô the Waters safely glide,
Not Birds unhurt are to fly o'r't allow'd.
The Towns beneath do yet their Beauty bear,
For they alas not Guilty were,
The Men did all the Sin and all the Judgment share.
Around th' Infectious Shore
Fair-Trees deceitfull Apples bore,
To th' Eye they did with ravishing Beauty shine;
(Such are the looks of Sin)
But Loathsom Dust and Ashes held within.

XXIII.

Sometimes in distant Realms I rove,
For Curiosity is unconfin'd;
Where Springs their Vigorous Source send out *above*,
Or where vast Rocks *below* their Streams do bind.
Where they, unseen by Mortal Eye,
The *Subterranean* Progeny do feed;
Or *Dæmons* of the Mines (if any such there be)
Or beneath Rocks Metallick Compounds breed.
Below the *Alps* now my Dark Course is led,
Where *PELION* upon *OSSA'S* thrown,

Where

Where Hills on Hills, Mountains on Mountains ſtand,
Till they to Heaven lift their Aſpiring Head;
And do not ſeem the Work of Nature's hand,
But broken Ruines of the former World. ——
The *Monſtrous Caverns*, that Vaſt Depths do hold,
In their wide Arms do Seas enfold.
Who can their ſecret Sources ſhow?
Whether they ſwell from melted Snow,
Which ever Crowns their Hoary Head:
Or whether from condenſed Air they'r bred,
In Great Vacuities below:
Or whether from the Sea their ſecret Courſe doth flow
The boundleſs Treaſure's in their Bowels laid,
The Minerals, that there abound,
And Richly pay for all the Barren Ground.

XXIV.

To all the Lakes from theſe Abyſſes bred,
By hidden winding ways I paſs'd:
Now I in *Switzerland* lift up my Head,
And trembling and agaſt
The barren Rocks and threatning Mountains dread:
Where Nature ſhows but a Step-Mother's Love;
Where the harſh Soil unkind doth prove;
Yet all is ſweetned by Bleſs'd *Liberty*.
Their rugged Rocks, that ſcarce their Toil repay,
Their Vales with headlong Torrents waſh't away,
They more do Prize than Dangerous State,
Than Smiling Treacherous Pageantry,
VVhile Peace and Safety do upon them wait.

XXV.

Now I i'th *Garden* of the VVorld do riſe,
The *Queen* of Nations *ITALY*,
And from a Lake behold the Country round,
Which doth with Nature's Gifts abound,

And only *Freedom* wants to mak't a *Paradise.*
But see the Dreadfull Curse of Tyranny!
The untill'd Soil doth Mourn its State,
Th' unpeopled Land a VVildernefs doth ly,
The wearied Peasant doth lament his Fate,
VVorks for what He ne'r enjoys;
But Groans, Sinks, and Expires beneath his Miseries.
Rapine and dire Oppression all doth seize,
And Curses, what God Blefs'd before.
In vain God Plenty sends, and Store,
If dire Exactions keeps the Subjects poor.
Adam from Paradise was driven; ——
And here Men fly the next Blefs'd Place to Heaven.

A *PINDARIQUE* Ode.

PART IV.

STANZA I.

NO Corner of the World my Course did miss:
Not the unconstant stormy *Irish* Seas,
Which even the *Adrian* Friths surpass:
Not Naked savage *Orcades*,
Nor *Thule*, which from *Rome* the Farthest lay
Of all the Islands, She found out i'th' Sea.
Not *Norway* Deeps, where the Prophetick Whale doth lie;
Till the approaching Destiny
Of Him, whom all the Nation doth obey,
Doth call him up from's solitary Room,
In Regions deep below, to tell the World the Doom.
Not the tempestuous Seas, where *Dæmons* dwell,
Where Spirits rule the Winds, and move the Sea
The Air and Ocean sway,
And *Lapland* Witches Winds do sell.

II.

Not Seas and Lands by Icy Mountains barr'd,
The Curse of Nature made in spight,
Where fearless Bears the Shoars do guard,
And like their Land are cloath'd in white.
Yet (so each One is to his Native Country kind)
Spight of th' Inclemencies of Soil and Wind,

The Region doth within possess
(Whom their own Land the best doth please)
An Olive-colour'd Race of Savages.
Nor could I without Pitty see
The poor Remains of Thee, Great *Willoughby!*
Whose Breast retain'd a Generous Fire,
Enough to' have thaw'd the Polar Ice:
But doom'd by the more rigid Destinies,
Disdaining thou by Night and Frost wer't forced to expire.
Thy shatter'd Hulk a Seamark lies,
And doth forbid farther Discoveries:
Nor th' unrelenting Element to dare,
That would not so much Vertue spare.

III.

Nor did I lose
The moving Sight of those,
That while they sought the happy Coast,
Where the Seas Bosom opens to *Cathay*;
I'th' unknown untrac'd way,
In spight o'th' *Zenith* Cynosure were lost.
Where broken Isles is all the Land,
Rough Icy Mountains all the Strand;
That scarce a Living Creature doth contain,
And (if ought be) doth seem by Nature made in vain.
Whose Seas do with the Land Resemblance hold,
Now an unfathomable Deep
And now a Shoaly Sea:
Now Rocks, that do forbid a VVay,
Now an Abyss Precipitous and steep:
Besides the lasting Curse of Night and Cold.
Nor, Daring *Gilbert*, was thy Tract yet lost;
When thou at *Newfound-land* took'st Seisure of the Coast.
Great the Designs, which did out-brave thy Fate,
Thou liv'st in Fame, and art than Destiny more Great.

IV.

By all the Coasts, that *English* Ships do plow,
VVhen they to fruitfull Colonies do go:
VVhere they the Skins of Beasts and Birds do wear,
VVhere they adorn'd with Feathers do appear,
And whe e in Cloaths of downy Moss they pride.
From hence my speedy Course did glide
To *Florida*, that ope's her beauteous Bosom wide.
Florida, the Scene of Blood,
That hath unconquer'd stood
By *Spanish* Rage, or *English* Courtesie.
By all the Coasts, that Gold so oft devours,
The gilded *Spanish* Shoars:
All the Rich Wrecks, that overspread the Sea,
All those in the *Campeche* Bay,
So oft inur'd to Pyracy;
VVhen *Boucaniers* their Pranks do play:
And what all Ills hath suffer'd, *PANAMA*;
The Glorious Island, once the Ocean's Pride,
That now a Wilderness doth lie:
Hispaniola, that did Empress ride;
The fatal Inlet into Slavery.
That first by ventrous Mariner was spy'd;
VVhen the despairing Fleet had else return'd,
VVhose Height so oft enslaved *India* mourn'd.

V.

By all the scatter'd Isles, that guard the *Western* Shoar;
VVhere barbarous *Cannibals* do on their Neighbours p
Who *Neptune's* bosom in their *Canoos* scour,
And bloody Teeth do on Men's Entrails lay;
Carouse in Enemies Blood,
And the yet-quaking Members make their Food
All, where the *Amazonian* River flows,
That from a thousand Streams renowned grows.

All, that the fair *Guiana* shows,
Immortaliz'd by *Raleigh's* Pen.
Or that, which hath its Name from *Plate*,
And groans so oft beneath the Precious weight:
All the Inhospitable Shores for Men,
Down to the dismall Straits of *Megallan*.

VI.

I found out all the Solitary Isles,
VVhere Uncorrupted Nature smiles,
Spread out in spacious Deeps alone:
That ne're to Knowledge were betray'd,
And happy, if they never be;
So blessed 'tis to be Unknown,
And ly from Danger, as Discovery, free!
Riches, when known, expose to Prey,
And Happiness, when envy'd, doth betray,
And to Invasion ope's a way.
Cut from the VVorld these nothing Dread,
But, thankfull, on what Nature gives, do feed.
Know but their own, and have no wild Desires,
Nor nourish in their Breast Tyrannick Fires.
Think, there's no VVorld but what they do enjoy,
Nor yet beyond their Coast their VVishes fly.
Blessed in *Peace*, and in unsullied *Joy*,
Bless'd in, the Crown of Blessings, *Liberty*:
Bless'd, that ne're long for Foreign Stores,
Nor foreign Vices nourish on their Shores!
Here fixt *Content* doth place her Seat,
Beyond ev'n Philosophick Notions Great.
Happy in Ignorance, they know no more,
Than Nature's humble Store;
Pleas'd with their state, they Strangers are to Care,
They nothing hope for, and they nothing fear.

VII.

All those, that far from Entercourse are laid,
And do just Admiration gain,
(Since they know none, and are to all unknown)
How Men and Beasts were into them convey'd.
Except they did remain,
When swallow'd Continents sunk down:
Or by *Angelick* Ministry the work was done.
Those, whom kind Nature doth bestow
To be the *Seaman's Guide* ;
And kind Refreshment to provide :
Where *Tortoyses* sweet Food to them allow,
Whom the salt Waves and salter Food had dri'ed
Where the salubrious Air
And limpid Water doth their broken Spirits cheer

VIII.

Nor did I miss the *Southern* unknown Coast,
That doth of boundless Riches boast ;
And dares the bold Discoverer:
Whose Virgin Soil ne're yet did Stranger bear,
Nor *European* Keel her Seas did ever tear.
Vast spacious Tracts that Coast shall once unfold,
Even to the *Southern* frozen Zone :
Which vainly now are judged Sea ;
(And so was once *America*)
As great, as are the Worlds already known ;
That yet in Darkness and Obscurity lie down.
That do invaluable Treasures hold
Of what, all Men adore, Eye-dazling *Gold*.

IX.

The quiet Waves of the *Pacifick* Sea,
Where seldom Tempests rage,
Or Storms with shatter'd Ships engage;
But Nature there in her Repose doth lie.

Where the Inhabitants of *America*,
That the *South* Sea enjoy :
Free from fear and from annoy,
Sleep on the Shore in soft security
With Bars of massy Silver by.
They leave their Ships at Ancker on the Shore,
Thó fraighted with inestimable Store,
And far within the Land themselves employ :
And neither Tempests fear nor Pyracy.
By all the Happy Coast I pass'd,
Happy in every thing, but Liberty :
Where yet the Marks of *DRAKE* and *CANDISH* last,
The scourges of the *Spanish* Pride.
I saw where the Vast *Carrack* once did ride,
Enrich'd with all the *Indian* Store,
Which Noble *CANDISH* by his Valour bore ;
And round the World in Triumph drew :
While trembling *Spain* lay gasping at the View.

X.

Hence thrô the Spacious Main,
The way, that our Great *Hero* went,
Along his shining Tract I ran
To every *Indian* Isle and Continent.
The Seas, that do embrace the *PHILIPPINES*,
Which Nature scattering o'r the Ocean throws :
That, which around *MALDIVA* shines,
Where the Sea-*Coco* under water grows,
And a Medicinal Juice for Poyson shows.
The Sea, that the *MOLUCCO* Isles confines,
Whose Fragrant Cloves the World do Store,
And th' Ocean do perfume, when out of sight of Shore.
Those, who their Parents, when they'r old, do eat,
Those, who the Fig-tree make their Meat,
Those, who from *Coco*-leaves their cloaths do get.

Lands,

Lands, that such Monstrous *Crabs* do breed,
That Men their Dangerous Neighbourhood do dread;
For what they grasp, they kill.
Those, who such Giant *Tortoyses* do find,
Ten Men their hollow Cavity can't fill,
But have at once within them din'd.
Thro all that Sea, that's thick with Islands sown,
And's Nature's Harvest when well grown,
My Vigorous Course did go------
From the Contemned Islands of the Main,
Which no distinctive Names do know,
To * *Sumatra*, the ancient *Taprobane*.

* So Mercator &c. *But others make* Zeilan, *as* Barrius *and* Vererius.

XI.

Nor did that Coast escape my View,
Whose Riches and unbounded Stores
From forreign Climes and distant Shores
So many Lovers drew:
The *Indian* Sea, where all the World doth greet,
The Center where from every part they meet:
The Sea, that ne'r doth rest,
Whom Tydes and Tempests break, but most the plowing Keels (molest:
The Shores, where Wives with their Dead Husbands burn,
And mix their Loving Ashes in one Urn.
Where Servants with their Masters die,
That in the other world they may not unattended be.
Where *Pythagoreans* do all Flesh forbear,
And whatsoe'r hath Life do spare:
That Lawn before their Faces wear,
Lest their unwary breath,
Should give a Fly or Insect Death.

XII.

Where *Brachman's* with a Stoical Pride
Do the extremity of Heat and Cold abide.

The

The Shore, where *Ganges* is ador'd,
And is with Pilgrims from all Quarters ſtor'd,
Who in his Waves do hope to waſh their Sins away:
Where they to Monſtrous *Pagods* pray,
Whoſe Dreadfull Looks do the Adorers ſcare,
And only can be worſhipped for fear.
Where Hoſpitals for Birds and Beaſts they build,
And buy their Lives off, when they'r to be kill'd.
The Barbarous Shore,
Where what they firſt at Morning meet, they all the Day a-
Or what the reſt in Folly doth excell, (dore.
Where they the *APES* Tooth worſhip, *PERIMAL*.
The Sea of *Bengala* inſlav'd to Luſt:
Or th' black-Mouth'd beardleſs *PEGUAN*:
Or where the KING can't his own Iſſue truſt,
But's Siſters Son doth after Reign.

XIII.

Nor could I miſs *Cape Comori*,
Where Mounts of Fruitfull Shell-fiſh ly,
That *Orient* Pearls do in their womb contain.
Where the bold *Indian* Jumps into the Main,
Doth down unto the Shining Bottom Dive,
That needs no Light, but what the Pearls do give,
That up a precious Load doth bear;
Unto the Sun and Air
The rugged *Oyſters* doth expoſe,
Whoſe Heat the Treaſures do diſcloſe.
While *SHARKS* and *HAVENS* wait
To bring the Wretch his Fate;
And with a Dire Revenge, repay
Th' Invaſion of their Element, the Sea.
Pearls the too Coſtly Price of Blood!
That neither Clothing can beſtow nor Food;

That one single Life can't buy,
Made not for Nature's wants, but Luxury.

XIV.

Nor did I the *Arabian* Gulph omit,
Where the *Impostor* doth in Triumph sit.
Nor yet that Sea, whose red Discolour'd Stream
To endless Disputation gives a Theam:
Which the *Jews* wondrous Passage tells,
And yet retains the Marks of *Pharaoh's* Chariot-wheel
But in the Tract, that *Solomon's* Ships did pass
My Course to *Sophola* did hold,
By Wise-Men thought th' *OPHIR* of old,
And yet Renown'd for Gold.
Whose Mines even Admiration do surpass:
Whose Buildings yet do Ancient Greatness bear,
Engrav'd with many an Antique Character.

XV.

Nor did I fear the Dreadfull *CAPE* to pass,
Of the known World the Farthest Part:
Where Storms and Thunder do make Nature start.
Where th' Elements do know no Peace,
Where Feuds and Quarrels never cease;
Whose Threatning Mountains have defy'd the Main,
That hath for many Ages beat in Vain
Those Adamantine Rocks, that yet its fury do restrain.
Twice I cut the Burning Line,
Where Perpendicular Rays do from the *Zenith* shine.
I swiftly pass'd th' Unnatural Shore;
Where Parents do their Children sell,
And Children cruelly do with their Parents deal.
Where *Niger's* Streams the Parched Fields restore,
And spight of the Sun's dazling Light
On every Face writes Night.

Nor did my Courſe the Wondrous Iſles forgo,
Where Weeping Trees bedew the Thirſty Plain,
And with their Fruitfull Drops ſupply the Place of Rain,
And *Phaethon's* Siſters in their Tears outdo.
And what no leſs a Wonder may appear,
Where Trees do Cluſtring Heaps of *Oyſters* bear.
To all the Scatter'd Iſles my Courſe I Steer,
Where groaning *Atlas* ſinks beneath his Weight;
All the Rude Coaſts to the *Herculean* ſtraight.

XVI.

Enterd; The Barbarous *Africk* Shore I ſpy'd,
Where once *Rome's* Emulous Foe with Haughty Pride
Lifted her Creſt on high:
Her very Ruines ruined
I could not without Indignation ſee,
That once ſtood Candidate the Univerſe to Guide.
Nor could I unſaluted *MALTA* paſs,
Where Valour doth Triumphant ſit,
And Rears on High the *Chriſtian* Name:
Once a Contemned Deſpicable Place,
Whoſe Barren Rocks, but for Sea-Monſters fit,
With Man could ſcarcely Friendſhip claim.
So Time and Change is over all things ſpread;
And that, which once liv'd High in Fame, lies Dead,
And what lay low in Duſt, exalts a Glorious Head.

XVII.

Malta, thou now art Darling Child of Fame;
Yet this unto thy Worth thou doſt not owe;
From thy Brave Valiant Sons thy Fame doth grow.
Regions and Citties are but Senſeleſs things,
Nor of themſelves Renown acquire;
The dull Groſs Matter wants an Actuating Fire:
And when they do to Noble Acts aſpire,

They owe the Motion to Great Captains, and to Valiant Kings.
'Twas not the Buildings made *Rome* Great,
Nor was't the *Capitol* the World obey'd:
Scipio and *Cæsar* did Her Fame create,
And Her *Commanders* Her to Grandeur led;
Their Conduct and the Souldiers Valour did erect Her State.

XVIII.

Greece yet remains; the Soil's the same,
In every Thing but *Men* and *Fame*;
The Ground, whereon She did her Citties raise,
With weeping Eyes yet Travellers do trace;
But oh! A Fatal Change from what it was.
Fruitfulness yet upon Her Bosom's spread,
And Plenty on Her Face doth smile:
But yet the *Quintessence* is fled;
The Change is in the *Men* and not the *Soil*.
The Men *Greece* Learned made,
They Her Repute for Valour rais'd:
They were the Souls, and when they fled,
The Carcasses Deformed lay and Dead:
Now *Cowardise* and *Ignorance* the Region hath debas'd.

XIX.

Nor know we Blessed Isle, but Thou
And *Venice*, which from small beginnings sprung,
As former Times did not your Glory know,
Which now's in Acts of Valiant Heroes sung.
When your Great Souls (as they) must once ly Dead
(The General Lot that haps to all;
If others rise not in their stead;)
In Fame, which is not to your Seats confin'd,
But's the Reflection of a Gallant Mind;
You may from your Exalted Stations fall:
And other Seats, that yet no Worth do show,

By

By Fate's unſeen Decree
May lift their low and obſcure Heads on high;
And from one HERO may Immortal grow:
As to *Epaminondas Thebes* her Name did ow.

XX.

I ſaw *Nile's* troubled Stream,
For Learned *Pens* a laſting Theme,
That doth bleſs'd Fruitfulneſs beſtow.
And the once Famous Road,
Where *Cæſar's* Navy ſtood;
When *Ægypt* did beneath his Scepter bow:
Where *Tyre* once did with Pride and Riches ſwell;
Now deſolate and Forlorn:
The Fam'd *SIGÆUM* Promontory, where
Homer's Immortal *Heroes* buried were.
Nor did I miſs the Bay,
Where once the *Græcian* Navy lay,
Whom *HECTOR's* Flames did burn.
With mixed Scorn and Anger I beheld
SCAMANDER's celebrated Stream,
So oft with *Greek* and *Trojan* Bodies fill'd;
Whoſe rapid Floods whole Armies bore away
Into the Neighbouring Sea:
(If We, what ancient *Bards* relate, eſteem)
Now a contemned deſpicable *Rill*,
Whom *Winter's* Rains do fill;
But *Summer* Heats doth of its Force bereave:
And thence doth Ground for our Suſpition give,
That all the *Celebrated Tale* was but a *Poet's* Dream.

XXI.

I view'd the Ports in *Hiſtory* Renown'd;
The States by laviſh *Poets* crown'd,
That did in Arts or Arms abound:

Once the World's Pride and now its Shame,
Which are in their dark Ruines sought in vain,
That even their very Shadows don't remain,
Mortal in(what they priz'd)ev'n their Immortal Name
Greece, that none Learn'd or Civil would allow,
To all the World is a *Barbarian* now.
The Seas, which once her numerous Ships did plow,
The *Sporades* i'th' the Ocean laid,
The Isles, that did to highest Splendour grow,
Now either Uninhabited,
Or else with Barbarism do lie o'respread :
That even, *Geographers* can scarce make good,
Where Learned *Athens*, or Voluptuous *Corinth* stood

XXII.

From these sad Objects I was call'd away
By a *Vulcano*, that arose
In an unfathomable Sea :
Or that the dreadfull Place of Punishment
Had there a Vent,
And did its furious Flames disclose :
Or that the *Subterranean* Heat
Had worn the Bounds so thin,
Had with such Force against the Barriers beat ;
They could not keep their eating Prisoners in :
Or that a sulphurous Mine took fire
And up unto the Stars the Seas did blow :
Or that some daring Engineer below
With his bold Art did up to Heaven aspire.

XXIII.

A sudden Fire from the Sea's Bottom broak :
The wrestling Elements the whole World shook.
Phœbus and *Neptune* ne're before
Did Martial up in Troops their Emulous Power :

Put in his Orb with Quiet bleſt
Each of his Realms the Rule poſſeſt.
The Government o'th' Sea the *Moon*
By ancient Right did own;
But, Lofty *Phœbus*, ne're before
Was *Tethys* thus ſubjected to thy Power;
Nor, except under thine Ambitious Son,
Suffer'd till now a Conflagration.
Water once rul'd the World: and once in Fire
Her old decaying Fabrick muſt expire.
When two ſuch Potent Foes do diſagree
How Dreadfull and Amazing muſt the Battel be?

XXIV.

A wide-ſtretch'd Mouth did vomit Thunder out,
Mountainous Stones from thence did fly,
As thô intended to Bombard the Sky.
In vain the Sea to quench the Furnace try'd,
Her Realm of Waves to get the Victory brought:
The Oiley Streams new *Pabulum* ſupply'd,
And ſulphurous Mines within did warlike Store provide.
Untill at laſt, when nought could part the Foes,
But Heaven and Earth ſeem'd at a loſs;
They of Themſelves, weary of ill-ſpent Store,
Did let the undecided Battle fall:
Reſign'd again the Claim to' each other's Power,
And Peace in Triumph did o're Earth and Sea inſtall.

XXV.

Thrô all the *TYRRHEN* and the *ADRIAN* Sea
I cut my untrackt Way:
And ſaw the Wrecks in their unrifled Bed,
By *Carthaginian* Ships or *Roman* made:
And could th' Antiquities, that there are laid,
By Art be thence convey'd,
How would they pleaſe the Curious Eye?
The Rarities what Sums could buy? XXVI. Not

XXVI.

Not *Hercules* Pillars could my Course confine,
I thrô the boundless *Ocean* steer'd,
And neither Storms nor Tempests fear'd:
The Marks of *Roman* Greatness view'd,
That all the *Northern* Continent subdu'd,
That did eternal Honour win:
Saw, where Great *Cæsar* first did trust the Sea,
When he design'd on *Brittany*;
And where his threatning Ships did stay.
The Noted *DOWNES*, the Seat of War,
That doth so oft engaging Navies bear:
Whose Bottom is an Armory,
That might an Iron Age supply;
Where Valiant *TRUMP* and *OPDAM* lie,
Whose gallant Acts a just Repute did gain:
In this ally'd to Immortality,
They were by Valiant *English* Heroes slain.
Happy; if other Foes they'd met i'th' watry Field!
Their *Genii* onely could to Nobler *Brittains* yield.

XXVII.

Nor could I, Noble *SANDWICH*, pass thy Fall,
For Evil Times too Brave a General!
Rumour (and who's from Malice free)
With pois'nous Lies had blasted Thee,
'Tis true thy Honour was above their Hate,
But Fame, that's priz'd by th' Generous and Great,
Unjustly Tax'd, fill'd thy Great Soul with Grief:
Nor could thy Prince's Kindness bring Relief.
No more, Proud *Dutch*, in your fam'd Victory pride;
He to his Countrymen his Ruine owes:
Who not by Valour, but by Treachery dy'd,
And not by *Dutch*, but by his *English*, Foes.

XXVIII. So

XXVIII.

So, my Wide Wishes satisfi'd,
Nothing unto my Daring Soul deny'd
Of all in which the Sea doth pride,
Neptune his Order did revoke,
The Charms, which made the Transformation, broke;
And Me my *Fishy Shape* forsook.
Bigg with desired Knowledge I regain,
The Nobler Form of Man:
And by the Sea-Gods Care,
From the dark Bottom, whence but Few return,
On *TRITONS* Backs I'm kindly born,
And with a Vigorous Warmth desire the upper Realms of Air.

The End.

CPSIA information can be obtained at www.ICGtesting.com
Printed in the USA
LVOW03s1813211214

419840LV00014B/414/P

9 781240 846252